P9-CFX-218

Classroom and Workshop-Tested Games, Puzzles, and Activities for the Elementary School

by Harriet Kinghorn

ere is a new volume chock-full of classroom-tested games, puzzles and activities that ake the "learning experience" in the elementary grades more "FUN" than work. Comled over a period of fourteen years, these classroom gems cut your planning workload half, while they provide a giant imaginative spark that turns any "dry" classroom vironment into a wonderland of learning.

PARTIAL OUTLINE OF CONTENTS

'EPPING ALONG IN READING AND TERATURE—Ways to make stories come ve • A list of art, writing and discussion eas for after a story • Supplementary games d aids to increase reading skills

CTATING AND WRITING ADVENJRES—How to set the environment for a riety of creative writing opportunities • eative nursery rhyme stories • Writing for purpose

RFORMING IN THE LOOKING GLASS deas for drama experiences • Flexible idelines for simple performances • How to ake props that create fun and interest • actical costumes

LT-BOARD ACTIVITIES THAT TEACH felt-board and some materials that adhere it • Felt-board activities encourage indendent learning • Math stories for the feltard

AMES FOR FUN AND LEARNING—eading and math games • Learning center mes that are simple to construct from rrow-aways" • Games that help spelling ills

AGIC MATHEMATICS—Activities using ometric shapes • How students can develop ncepts of money, time, temperature and easurement

WONDERS IN SCIENCE—"Glurtch": an exciting new mysterious formula for pupils to make • Recycling activities • "Guess my secret" game

JOURNEY IN SOCIAL STUDIES—Learning through an imaginary travel agency • Ways to learn about children of other lands • Careers • "Economics at work" • "A guided tour" • A map activity • Something old-something new file

CREATIVE ART EXPRESSIONS—A list of media for the art center • "Revolving art ideas" • "Three-dimensional standups" • How to use pencil shavings for art • Coffee monochromatics • Art expression with scraps

RECYCLING INTO CRAFTS—Fresh ideas for inexpensive craft projects • How to make crafts from throw-aways • Gifts • "Soap bottle viewer"

EXPERIENCES IN COOKING AND SEWING—Teaching initial sounds with food • A variety of simple cooking and sewing suggestions • Recipes created for individualized cooking • Recipes for candy, caramel corn, punch, and cracker treats

POT-POURRI—Suggestions for birthdays • How to motivate with stickers • Gift cards • A list of spare time activities • Wishes that come true

ABOUT THE AUTHOR

HARRIET KINGHORN has taught Kindergarten through fourth grade over a period of fourteen years. In 1973 she received the coveted "Outstanding Elementary Teachers of America Award." At present, Mrs. Kinghorn serves as the East Grand Forks representative on the Council on Admission to Professional Education, the local committee on The Right to Read, and the Continuing Education Committee. She has also written several articles for *The Instructor,* and has conducted a number of workshops for teachers.

Classroom and Workshop-Tested
Games,
Puzzles,
and
Activities
for the Elementary School

Classroom and Workshop-Tested Games, Puzzles, and Activities for the Elementary School

Harriet Kinghorn

Parker Publishing Company, Inc.
West Nyack, New York

Library of Congress Cataloging in Publication Data

Kinghorn, Harriet,
Classroom and workshop-tested games.

1. Educational games. 2. Creative activities and seat work. I. Title.
LB1029.G3K56 372.1'3 74-19394
ISBN 0-13-136309-3

Printed in the United States of America

To Norton, Michael, Cara, and Mary

Foreword

"Would you tell me, please," said Alice, lost in Wonderland, "which way I ought to go from here?"

"That depends a good deal on where you want to get to," said the Cheshire Cat.

"I don't much care where . . ." said Alice.

"Then it doesn't matter which way you go," said the Cat.

" . . . so long as I get somewhere," Alice added as an explanation.

"Oh, you're sure to do that," said the Cat, "if you only walk long enough."

This book is full of ideas that have taken some 15 years to "get somewhere." They are ideas that have in some way turned the drab world of beige and blackboard, at least for an hour or two, into Wonderland. The Wonderland thus created at those magic times, has been woven of many strands—the child's imagination, a teacher's ability to coax and encourage it, and materials in which it found its expression.

And now that the ideas contained herein have arrived somewhere, we find that that maddest of all creatures, the Cheshire Cat (the writer's apologies to the Hatter) was right all the time: "It does not matter which way you go"; and we add, "What matters is the journey itself—the wonders along the way."

The author would be claiming too much for her book if she said that every project or activity in it were a door to Wonderland or a trip through the Looking Glass; but she does believe that each is a first step along the way. It remains for those teachers who use this book to make possible a second step; and then, in all likelihood, those who will ultimately benefit—the children—will take steps three and four and so on the journey.

(By this time the reader has doubtless noticed the curious tone of this Foreword and has probably already distinguished the writer of the Foreword from the author of the book. The writer of the

Foreword has observed the book in the making for a long time and therefore is able to offer a different perspective on these materials —and perhaps a more objective one. And that is why it is he, and not the author, who addresses the reader here. Objectivity in this matter is no small accomplishment: the writer has had to get used to breathing the rarified air of Wonderland on a daily basis; he has had to get used to coming home and finding his wife sitting in the kitchen contemplating a paper plate full of soggy watermelon seeds or used coffee grounds or seeing an empty plastic container as a creature newly arrived from a fairy tale or nursery rhyme. He has been at times on the verge of walking back through the door from whence he came, to look for the piece of magic mushroom or the antidote to the magic elixer that has turned his house into a strange, if wonderful, place.)

From all this "introductory-to-the-introduction" the reader may extract a philosophy of elementary teaching or learning if he wishes, though *no one* philosophy has been intended. The author will provide here a collection of projects, games, instructional aids, bulletin boards, felt board activities, and "creative" pot-pourri. These "things" (there is no adequate cover term for them) are all for children; they are, in the main, self-directing, and thus can serve to relieve the busy teacher as well as to help the teacher who wishes to "open" her classroom all or part of the time.

Paradoxically, projects such as these will not relieve the teacher of any responsibility; indeed, she may find herself with a greater responsibility. If there is a tenet of pedagogy lurking in this book it might be stated something like this: The teacher (the one indispensable school fixture) must be awake and watching, always. When a youngster reveals an interest in something—be it brickbats, baseball, or ballet—the teacher should be prepared to nourish that interest, to encourage it to grow, expand, shift. This kind of approach is antithetical to the year's supply of prepared bulletin boards or inflexible textbooks or fading ditto masters. Indeed, tomorrow's activities may arise in part from today's playground chatter.

It is rare to find a teacher who has sufficient time to be flexible and still to pursue the goals set for her class. Thus, the items in this book are intended to be a store of ideas to help the over-burdened teacher *adapt to her students*. It is not intended by the author that her ideas be the end of anything; these ideas are open-ended: they will suggest still other activities; they can be modified by both teacher and children. Perhaps the teacher will learn much from her students, who, if encouraged, will seek out analogs. One activity will suggest another which may in turn bring on still another, especially if two or more children collaborate. Children have a natural ability to seek out similarities and differences that adult minds, cluttered with worries and anxiety, strictures and structures, do not have.

These beginning steps to Wonderland are, in a way, subversive. Lurking behind the strange sights and creatures, behind the pumpkin seeds and trash, are the cherished skills and facts that none of us is willing to admit are unimportant. Thus, some of these projects encourage careful observation; others allow the child to explore and discover; still others require manipulation skills, reasoning, reading, writing. Many of the projects allow the child to seek out means of self expression and outlets for the creative urge. Many of the projects encourage such social virtues as mutual respect, sharing, and, perhaps, simple kindness and understanding for each other.

Finally, the goal of this book has not been so much to add either material or activity to the classroom as to use to the fullest extent those things and activities that are already there. The author subscribes to the dictum that there is no such thing as "junk." Most of these projects and activities use materials that are already available in elementary schools; and many rely on the use of household "trash," which usually gets sent to the dump or down the disposal. In a way, the book suggests a kind of "creative recycling" and sets children and teachers to the task of seeking wonders in common things.

Perhaps the most important aspect of this book is the unusual way of looking at the world that is suggests. You may not wish to *use* any part of this material exactly as it is presented here; after all, you may have a more definite idea than Alice of where you want to get. It is the hope of the author that her book will suggest the sorts of things you might wish to see along the way.

Norton D. Kinghorn

How to Make Practically Everything from Practically Nothing at All

Over the last few years I have conducted in-service workshops, finding experienced teachers as well as new teachers are continually searching for practical new ideas and activities for their classes.

> "I need manipulative aids for my learning centers"; "I need activities that will encourage children to work independently, games that will develop reading and math skills, and ideas for small group projects"; "I need directions for puppets that children can make by themselves and some suggestions for throw-away materials that children can bring from home"; "I need flannel board and bulletin board ideas that will stimulate student participation"; "I need ways of involving my students in creative writings, drama, and art"; "I need more practical ideas for activities in all subject areas"—these are only a few of the needs expressed by teachers.

This handbook meets these needs. The games, puzzles, and other activities evolved out of my classroom and workshop experiences, and they are flexible enough to be adapted to various levels according to the individual needs and interest of the students. Many of the ideas relate to more than one subject area so, with very little modification, the projects can be used in different environments to develop a variety of skills. The easy-to-follow directions, the many illustrations, the free or inexpensive materials, the simple game and puppet patterns, and the examples of children's work will all help you plan these activities in no time at all. Whenever advance preparations are required, the directions are separated from the in-class activities.

Whenever you feel a need for more creative learning activities, you will find this book to be a practical and helpful guide to becoming a more knowledgeable resource teacher. It will give you and your students an opportunity to participate in a variety of exciting and individualized experiences, and many of these experiences will stimulate them to create similar activities for themselves and their classmates.

Harriet Kinghorn

ACKNOWLEDGMENTS

I wish to express my appreciation to the following people who helped in the preparation of the book: to Marcia Miller, Marjorie Rohlfs, and Linda Klabunde for their suggestions; to Julie Schoen for the illustrations; to Jean Anderegg and Janice Langemo for their help in revising the manuscript; to my student teachers, Peg Hawbaker and Melody Boyle, for their willingness to test some of the ideas; to Kent Anderson for photos; to my fellow teachers for their interest and support; and, finally, to the students whose creative talents are reflected on many pages of this book.

Contents

Chapter I

Stepping Along in Reading and Literature

AFTER THE STORY

The plot, characters, and style of the classroom story become more meaningful when students are given the opportunity to choose and to participate in a related activity after the story.

General Materials: story book, tape or a record of a story

Art Materials for Related Art Activities: general art supplies (see art supplies in Chapter 9). Special materials that relate to the specific story such as feathers for a story about a bird. (See more suggestions for related materials under "Surprise Kits" in this chapter.) Chart of art suggestions such as the chart that is given later in this section.

Drama Materials: large paper or an available blackboard for background scenery, if needed. Simple costumes and property. (See Chapter 3 for ideas.)

Discussion Materials: tape recorder, chart of suggestions for discussions, such as the one that is given later in this section.

Writing Materials: pencil and paper, chart of suggestions for writing, such as the one that is given later in this section.

Directions:

Set up the centers with appropriate materials. One child may be designated as the chairman of each group. For example, the discussion group chairman can be in charge of the tape recorder and lead the discussion questions.

After the students hear a story, they break into groups and each selects and develops an art, drama, discussion, or writing project. (The teacher moves from center to center to give help, if needed.) After projects are completed, each group may share their projects with other classmates.

This mural was made by the River Heights second graders after hearing the story of "The Doughnuts" from *Homer Price* by Robert McCloskey.

Art Chart

(Suggestions for "After the Story" and/or for choice cards in the "Surprise Kits.")

Make:

1. anything you wish relating to the story.
2. one or more of the characters out of clay.
3. a picture about the story.
4. puppets of the characters in the story—of sack, paper towel, interfacing, stick, or box, or any other kind.
5. a colored chalk picture about the story.
6. an illustration of a scene that the illustrator could have included in this book, but didn't.
7. a poster advertising this book.

8. one or more characters from cardboard or oaktag. Design various clothes that the characters might wear from interfacing fabric, wallpaper, or some other suitable material.
9. a sequence of illustrations about the story to slide through a milk carton viewer.
10. a mural illustrating the book. (A friend may work with you.)
11. a mobile about this story.
12. a panorama about this book. (A shoe box or other suitable box needs to be available.)
13. a book jacket for this story.
14. a bulletin board display based on this story. (A small bulletin board needs to be available for this activity.)
15. a decorated paper plate that will relate in someway to this story.
16. a picture about this story from scrap materials.
17. a paper mosaic picture or design about this story.
18. an illustration of the scene you enjoyed the most.
19. a picture with yarn or string.
20. a tissue paper picture.
21. a picture with crayons on a piece of sandpaper.
22. something pertaining to the story out of the materials in the "recycling box."
23. a sponge painting about the story.

Add, modify, or omit to make this chart suitable to fit your classroom needs.

Discussion Chart
(Suggestions for "After the Story")

1. Who is your favorite character in this story?
2. What is your favorite part of the story?
3. Why do you like or dislike this story?
4. Where did the story take place? If possible, find the location on the map.
5. Retell the beginning of this story.
6. Retell the ending of this story.
7. Imagine that you are one of the characters in this story. As this character, tell something about yourself.
8. How would you change the story if you were the author?

9. If we were to act out this story, what character would you like to be? Why?
10. Think of a different beginning for the story and discuss your idea.
11. Think of a different ending for the story and discuss your idea.
12. Think of different titles that might be used for this story and discuss your ideas.
13. Imagine that you are the author of this story. Why did you write it?
14. Discuss the way that this story makes you feel. Why?
15. Can you make up a different story using these same characters?

Writing Chart

(Suggestions for "After the Story" and/or for choice cards in the "Surprise Kits.")

Write:

1. whatever you wish to tell about the story.
2. one or more riddles about this story that you might ask others who also read the story.
3. some questions that you might ask some friends who had read this book, too.
4. in your own words, the part of the story that you think is the funniest.
5. in your own words, about the most exciting part of this story.
6. in your own words, about the saddest part of the story.
7. about one or more of the characters. Make them come alive!
8. some questions that you might ask one of the characters if you were visiting with this person.
9. your own beginning to this story.
10. your own ending to this story.
11. about how you could change this story.
12. a television script based on your favorite part of this book.
13. a radio version of your favorite part of the book.
14. a movie script for part, or all, of this book.
15. a short pamphlet that you might use to advertise this book if you were the publisher.

16. a radio or television announcement to advertise this book.
17. this story so that a different character (either a person or an animal) is telling the story.
18. a different title for this story.
19. a puppet show based on your favorite part of this book to present to some classmates.
20. a letter to a friend to tell him about this book.
21. about the part of the book you liked best.

FENCE IN THE ANIMALS

This activity is a simple but very effective way of teaching children to recognize the names of animals. Language development takes place as the students fence in different animals.

Materials Needed: oaktag or corregated border paper, three dimensional plastic farm animals, scissors, marking pen

Preparations:

1. Make a simple fence from oaktag with a separate section for each kind of animal.
2. Write the name of a different animal on each section of the fence (corresponding to the available plastic animals.)
3. Make a barn from a box, if desired.
4. See riddles in back of this section for readers.

Directions:

Place each animal inside the proper section of fence by matching the animal to the word on the fence.

Cards with a riddle or short paragraph about each animal are used for those who can read. Children read cards, then place the animal in the proper section of the fence. For example,

> I have two eyes, two ears, four legs, and a long swishing tail. I say "Moo." Put me in my pen.

Variations:

1. Zoo animals and cages (might use strawberry cartons) can easily be used in this activity.
2. Some children enjoy the opportunity to dictate or write the riddles for this activity.

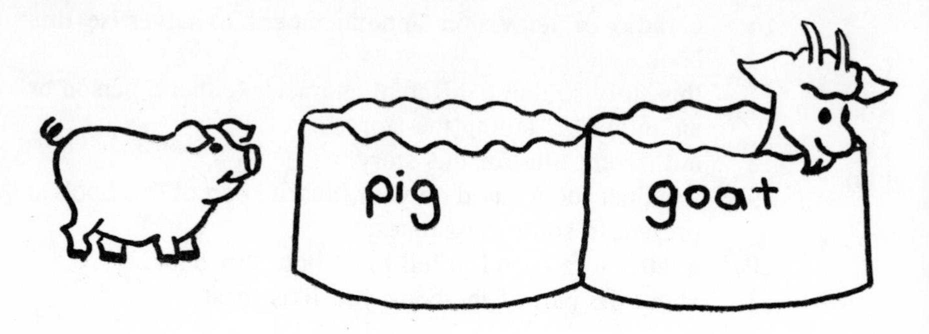

Farm Riddles by Melody

I have a funny nose. My tail is curly. Put me in my pen. (Pig)

I have four legs and a long tail. I give you something to drink. Put me in my pen. (Cow)

I have two feet. I can swim and I say, "Quack." Put me inside the fence. (Duck)

I have four legs and a mane. Sometimes I am stubborn and sometimes I kick. Put me in my pen. (Mule)

I have two legs and I like corn. I say "Cock-a-doodle-doo." Put me inside the fence. (Rooster)

I am a baby. My mother is a cow. Put me in my pen. (Calf)

I have four legs and two ears. I am wooly. Put me inside the fence. (Sheep)

I am a baby. My mother likes to carry people on her back. Fence me in! (Colt)

I have two legs. I am often eaten at Thanksgiving. Put me inside the fence. (Turkey)

I have four legs and whiskers. I also have two horns. Put me in my pen. (Goat)

I have four legs and a mane. My tail is long and my feet have hooves. I whinny and often run in races. Put me inside the fence. (Horse)

I am a baby. I have four feet. I say, "Baa, baa." Put me in my pen. (Lamb)

I am a baby. I have two legs and yellow feathers. I say "Peep, peep." Put me in my pen. (Chick)

HOUSE OF WORDS

Why not recycle a small milk carton into a house that holds words? Students enjoy reading as they pull words from the house. This is an excellent way to check and to help each student with the words that give him difficulty.

Materials Needed: small milk carton, shelf paper or some other suitable paper to cover carton, white glue, scissors, long strips of paper with words typed horizontally across the paper, marking pen or crayons

Preparations:

1. Open the milk carton at the top and cover all sides with paper.
2. Cut a horizontal slot near the bottom of the milk carton so that strips of paper can easily slide through it.
3. Type desired words in columns on ditto master, duplicate, cut and paste columns into one long strip.
4. Roll up strip of paper and place it inside the house.
5. Design windows and doors with marking pens and add a red clothespin chimney, if desired.

Directions:

A child pulls one word at a time from the house and tells the word to a teacher or older student. He may continue until he

misses one. When he misses a word, he cuts off the list at that point. He reviews the word that he missed and waits for another turn. When he has gone through the entire list correctly, he may earn a sticker.

JINGLES

This activity is designed to encourage audience participation in storytelling. Children become directly involved in the story when they are asked to supply a missing rhyming word and complete each of the jingles. Some children will have fun making their own jingles and/or drawing their own illustrations.

(A child-participation story)

"Mother, look what Kent helped me to make." Kendra came running from the kitchen with the toy in her hand.

Mrs. Moore put down her dust rag and turned to examine the object that her small daughter had thrust under her nose. It was a paper sack, with an owl face painted on one side.

"And look, Mommy," said Kendra as she turned the sack upside down, "We can stuff it with paper to make a stuffed toy."

"Why Kendra, that's very nice. Why don't you. . ." Just then a voice interrupted her.

"Mother! Kendra! Come quick!" Kent called to them anxiously. "Come and see what a terrible thing Flaps has done!"

Mrs. Moore and Kendra hurried into the toyroom to see what all the excitement was about. "What a sight!" exclaimed Mother, as she gazed at the toyroom floor. Pieces of stuffed animals were scattered all around the room. Each toy had been chewed and torn by the dog.

"Bad dog," cried Kent, shaking his finger at the frightened dog.

"Oh, this is terrible. Our toys look so sad," said Kendra, with tears in her eyes.

Mother put her hand on Kendra's shoulder. "Well, if we all get to work, we can soon make the animals look happy again," said Mother. "My, it looks like Flaps has torn every single one. Kent, let's have you tell us which part of each toy is missing, Kendra will hunt for it, and I'll find some way of mending it."

"Okay," said Kent, stooping over to pick up the toy deer which was lying near his foot.

Kent made the work go faster by making up a jingle for each toy. Mother and Kendra added to the fun by saying the missing word at the end of each jingle. Perhaps you would like to join Mrs. Moore and Kendra in the jingle game, too.

Dear, little deer, Your're missing an ___. (ear)

Mr. Seal doesn't act so chipper
Since he has lost his flappy___. (flipper)

It's certainly plain
That pony lost his ___. (mane)

Raggedy Ann might cry and cry
With only one black shoe-button ___. (eye)

Our Ducky Lill
Has lost her ___. (bill)

Camel is down in the dumps
Because he has lost his ___. (humps)

Jumbo's just sunk
Without his ___. (trunk) *elephant*

Oh Mrs. Cow, as quick as a flash,
Puppy pulled out your pretty eye___. (lash)

I made my kitty from a white stuffed sack,
And Flaps has torn its paper___. (back)

My poor unhappy crocodile,
You almost lost your big wide___. (smile)

Did that dog wipe
Our little skunk's ___? (stripe)

Monkey can't swing on a rail
If we don't find his curly___. (tail)

Poor Joey doesn't have a couch,
His Mother has lost her cozy___. (pouch)

You can't swim a race and win,
If puppy has your slippery___. (fin) *fish*

Spotted Giraffe, have you been torn?
Why yes, I see, you're minus a___. (horn)

Teddy Bear, Teddy Bear, we'll end with you, sir.
All we need now is your piece of soft ___. (fur)

OPPOSITES

This activity is intended to teach and/or reinforce the concept of "opposite." The children explore the meaning of "opposite" as they try to illustrate this concept in their own art work.

Materials Needed: paper, crayons or paints

Directions:

Children can easily work on this activity independently after the word "opposite" has been discussed. Each child draws whatever picture he chooses on paper. On the other side of this paper he draws the *opposite* of the first picture.

Variation:

Tell the children to keep their "opposite" pictures a secret so that they may play a game. Each child shows his picture to a small group who try to guess what is on the opposite side of the paper.

SURPRISE KITS

Surprise your students by making "Surprise Kits" for them. These kits are a means of individualizing reading and motivating students to respond to books. The children will surprise you with their ingenuity in making interesting art projects from the throw-aways in their kits.

Materials Needed: a large manuscript envelope for each student, a book (or story on a sheet of paper) for each student, selected according to his level of reading, various types of art materials

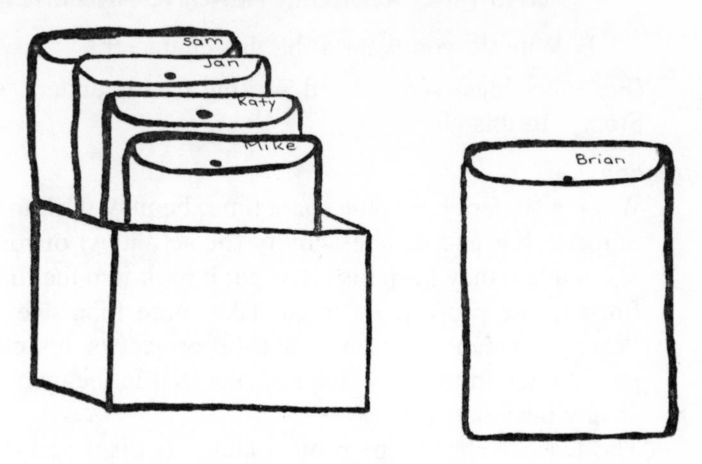

for a story-related art experience, a box for filing envelopes, a Choice Card for each envelope (optional—see example under preparations). Background paper should be available to students in or out of the kit.

Preparations:

1. Write a student's name, last name first, at the top of each envelope so the envelopes can be easily alphabetically filed in a box.
2. In each envelope put writing paper and various types of materials that might inspire a student art project.
3. (Optional) A Choice Card for each envelope is made by listing two or three different story-related activities. The student has an opportunity to choose the activity (or activities) that he prefers. These activities vary from one story to another. The same ideas may be used on choice cards for different kits as long as they are geared to each child's level of learning. An example of a Choice Card is as follows:

Choice Card

Do one, two, or all of the following activities:

1. Write to a friend and tell your friend something about this story.
2. Create a picture or design about this story.
3. Answer the following questions:

   A. If you were to act out this story, what character would you want to be in the play?

B. Why do you want to be this character?

(For other ideas see Art and Writing Charts under "After the Story" in this chapter.)

Directions:

When a student has some spare time, he may wish to open his Surprise Kit and do the activity (or activities) of his choice. The student may keep his kit or put it back into the file until he finishes the project. (It might take more than one session.) When a student has completed the project of his choice, he puts it back in the envelope and places it in the teacher's desk or any designated place.

The teacher checks the project and it is displayed or handed back to the student. The envelope is refilled with a different book, Choice Card, and writing and art materials.

Then the kit is placed back in the file, ready for another surprise experience.

Variations:

1. Two or three questions about the story can be asked before choices are listed.
2. Poems may be used instead of stories.
3. Surprise Kits can be designed for experiences in other skills and subject areas.

This picture was made after reading *Mop Top*.

This picture was made after reading *Mickey's Magnet*.

Note:

Since the Surprise Kits are designed for independent use, the vocabulary and skills need to be introduced before they are listed as an activity on the Choice Card. For example, a student should be experienced in writing a letter before it is listed as an activity in the Surprise Kit.

Suggestions for Art Material in Surprise Kits

Stories (Use one or two suitable items in each kit)
About:

Apples Apple Jacks (cereal), apple seeds, cranberries
Ballons cellophane, vinyl cloth, pieces of balloon
Bears fake fur, velvet, pom-poms
Birds feathers, string, twine, grain, birdseed
Bubbles transparent plastic, cellophane
Butterflies tissue paper, net, wallpaper, pipe cleaners
Cat calico, broom straws, fake fur, yarn
Desert sandpaper, salt, sand
Dogs fake fur, plastic eyes, buttons
Doughnuts Cheerios (cereal)
Elephant grey suede, velvet, straws
Fence rick-rack, corregated paper, yarn, pipe cleaners
Fishing net, straw, stick, tiny lid
Flowers floral wallpaper, grass, pipe cleaners, tissue paper, scented drawer paper
Horses velvet, yarn, string, buttons, leather pieces
Magnet small piece of magnetic tape, paper clip
People interfacing fabric, yarn, buttons, sequins
Rabbit cotton, velvet, fake fur
Rain foil, cellophane
Seal black Contact paper, vinyl paper
Snow sago, rice, oatmeal
Stars paper stars in small plastic bag or box
Turtle small paper plate, lid
Vehicles buttons, reinforcement rings

Wood wood, Contact paper or vinyl cloth that resembles wood

Zoo Animals fake fur, carpet pieces, piece of plastic fruit carton

(See "Art Supplies" in Chapter 9 for further suggestions)

TEXTURED LETTERS

The sounds of the letters in the alphabet are more easily learned when the three-dimensional texture on each letter suggests its function. Glued to each of these textured letters is a material (not pictures) which begins with the same sound that the letter represents. Children get directly involved as they plan, discover, and design these letters with the appropriate textures. It is an informal and fun way to teach sound discrimination of letters.

Materials Needed: construction paper or tagboard, white glue, a different three-dimensional item for each letter of the alphabet

Directions:

Trace and cut out each letter of the alphabet. Discuss the materials that can be glued on each letter to represent the sound of that letter (a few at a time). Glue on a material which begins with the sound of the letter. For example, buttons can be glued on the letter "B" because the word "button" begins with "B." When digraphs and blends are presented, appropriate items can be glued on the letter combination, such as Cheerios to represent the beginning sound, "ch" of Cheerios.

Children bring materials and glue them onto letters that they have traced and cut out. (Pictures are not three-dimensional so they should be omitted.)

Variations:

1. Paste letters on large poster board for a textured alphabet collage.
2. Make up games to play with the texture board.

Materials for Textured Blends and Digraphs

dr —dress, drape material, drum (toy), dropper
cl —clips, clothespins, cloth, clay
wh—wheels, whistle
st —stars (paper), stamps, stickers
ch —cherry pits, Cheerios, chains, chalk

BCDFGHJ
KLMNPQR
STVWXYZ

sl —slate
pl —plastic, Play-doh, plum seeds
cr —Crackerjacks, crayons, cranberries
bl —black crayon, blue crayon, blouse, blanket, blotter
gr —grapes, grass
br —branch, bricks, broom straws, brown crayon
str —straws, string, strap
fl —flowers, flags
gl —glue and/or glitter, (doll) glasses
tw —twine, twigs
qu —quilt pieces
sm—Smacks (sugar cereal)
tr —truck (toy), trinkets
pr —prune seeds
ph —phone (toy)
pl —plastic, platter (toy)
sn —snaps
sh —shells, ship (toy), shoe string
sw—swing (toy), sweater (doll)
sc —scarf (doll), scraps of paper
thr—thread
th —thimble
spr—springs
sp —spoon, spaghetti

WORD BOARDS

Children help each other expand their vocabularies by creating these practical and manipulative word boards. The students can work on them independently in school or at home.

Materials Needed: posterboard or a sheet of cardboard covered with colored construction paper, marking pen or crayon, materials that describe the word written on Word Board

Preparations:

1. Write a word such as "transparent" on the Word Board with a marking pen or crayon.
2. Fold up the bottom of the board and staple at each end to make a pocket, as seen in illustration, or use brads or picture hangers to hold items. Some items can be glued directly on the board.

Directions:

Students supply materials from home or school that in some way describe the word on the board. For example, transparent materials are glued on "transparent" board. Then students might make "translucent" and "opaque" word boards.

Students can suggest words or choose words from the dictionary that would make interesting and meaningful word boards.

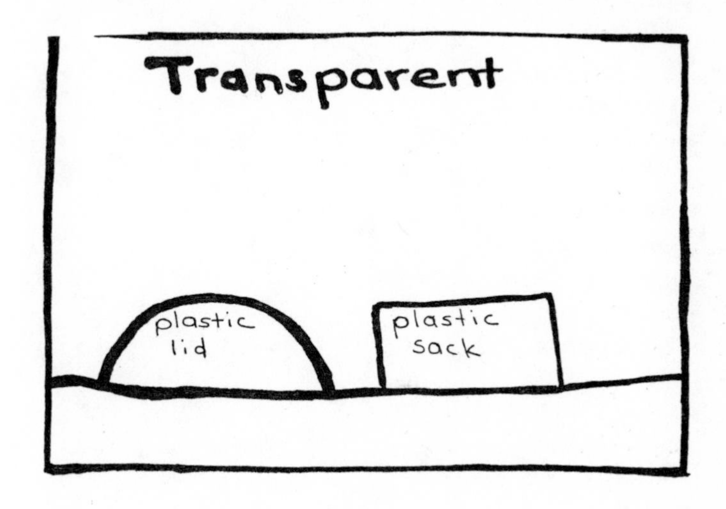

Chapter 2

Dictating and Writing Adventures

A WRITING LABORATORY

Students of all ages enjoy a writing laboratory filled with various types of objects to write and learn about.

Materials: shelf and/or table for objects, writing paper, pencils, crayons, scissors, magazines, a chart of story titles, poem file, list of most commonly misspelled words, dictionaries, and items such as maps, postcards, seeds, plants, toys, puppets, and animals

Preparation: Teacher and students discuss and find available objects to place in the laboratory. (See other writing ideas in this section.)

Directions: Some students may choose to sit by the table and write about an object that's in the laboratory while other students may choose to check out objects to take back to their seats to write about.

Two fifth grade girls made some characters from fake fur and then wrote the following story about them:

The Fuzz Family

Mr. Fuzz is blue. His wife is red. They have two purple kids. Their names are Fuzzy and Fluffy. They live in a cottonball house on Fuzzy Lane.

One fuzzy day a disease started in Fuzzville. Everyone got it. Even the mayor. The disease was called Fuzzlessidess. It meant that you lose your fuzz. Everyone lost their fuzz. Fluffy and Fuzzy didn't want to lose their hair. They decided to run away. So they packed all their bags and in the middle of the night they snuck out the door.

"It's scary out here," said Fuzzy.

"I know," said Fluffy, "but we must keep going."

They walked all night and in the morning they reached a town called Japanan. Nobody had fur on. Not anybody.

Fluffy and Fuzzy wondered if they had all come down with fuzzlessidess. But they were real people.

Fluffy went up to a man and said, "Did everyone in Japanan get fuzzlessidess?"

The man just looked at Fluffy. Then finally he spoke up, "We never had fuzz in the first place."

"What do you mean?" spoke up Fuzzy.

"Just what I said," answered the man.

The man walked away and Fluffy and Fuzzy just looked at each other. Never had fuzz! Wow! They had never heard of anyone not having fuzz.

All of a sudden Fuzzy felt homesick.

"I want to go home," said Fuzzy.

"Me too," said Fluffy. So they started for home. When they reached home they ran into the house to see if their parents looked any different. They didn't. The disease was all over!

Karin and Cara

CREATE AND WRITE

It is easy to correlate creative writing with art projects. In this activity, paper designs that the children cut out and unfold are the basis for original stories.

Materials Needed: various colors of construction paper, writing paper and pencils, scissors, glue, crayons (optional for each child)

Directions:

Each child folds a sheet of paper in half and cuts out two to four shapes, keeping part of each design on the fold. (Choose a paper of one color for the foreground and a paper of a contrasting color for the background.) He then pastes the designs on a background, using crayons to add details, if desired.

The child writes a story that relates to his art project.

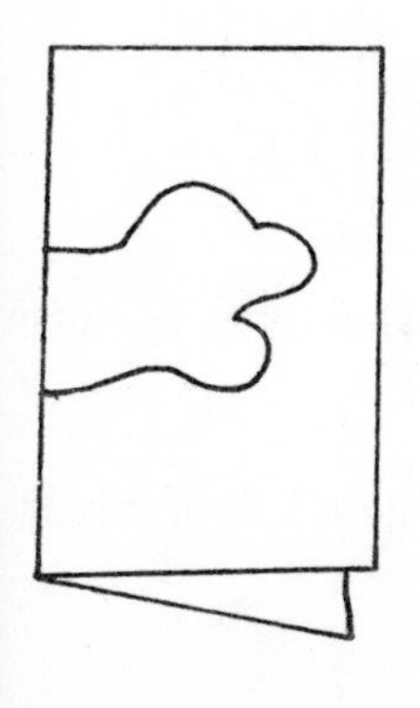

CREATIVE NURSERY RHYME STORIES

Nursery rhyme stories encourage thinking and/or writing from volunteers who enjoy using the familiar characters as a basis for their own stories.

Materials Needed: tape recorder or pencil and paper

Directions:

A student selects a nursery rhyme which he retells in a new version of his own invention. Students may record, write, or tell their stories. Some students may also illustrate their stories which can then be collected in a class creative story booklet.

The following is a nursery rhyme story which was created by a five year old who dictated it into a tape recorder. It was then transferred onto paper by the teacher:

Jack-Be-Nimble Story

One day Jack went in his house and Mommy had to go to the store. So he stayed home and stayed home and waited and waited. And then . . . he had a idea how to play a nursery rhyme so he got a little candle from his mommy and got the plate where they put big candles. And then lighted it with his own matches and then jumped over it. He got burned. So he went to put some different pants on, almost just alike, but not just alike, so he didn't. And he got off cause his mother was here. He took the candle off, quick unlighted it as it was, and took the holder back where it was. Then his mommy came in and said, "Have you had a good time?"

He said, "Yes." That's all.

The following story is typed exactly as a second grader wrote it:

"Jack benimel Jack be quick. Why did you jump over the candle stick?"

"Because my mommy told me to."

DESCRIPTION FUN

You may get to know your students better after this activity because the project calls for each child to describe himself.

Materials Needed: one sheet of writing paper, large sheet of paper, crayons, glue

Directions:

Fold a large sheet of paper in half. Each child writes a description of himself on the writing paper (without mentioning his name). The writing paper is then glued on front of the child's folded paper. The child draws a picture of himself on the inside and prints his name.

The teacher might read each description aloud and have the children guess who it is, if the children desire. If you can not guess the author from his own description, the picture and name provide the answer.

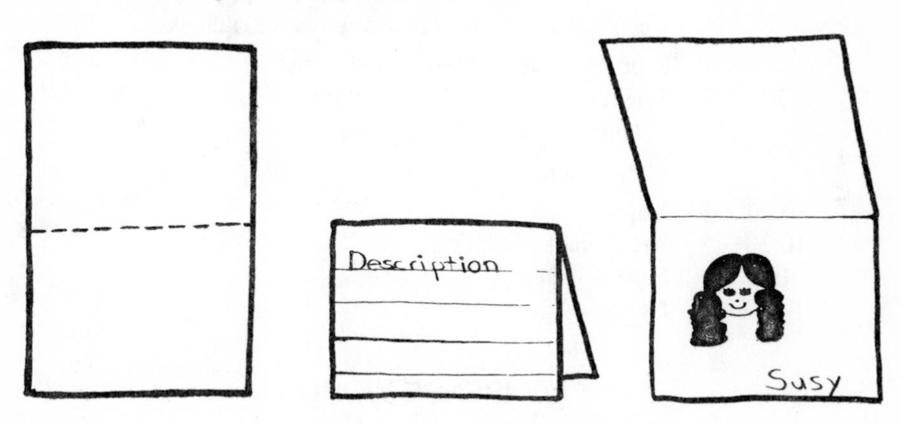

IMAGINARY TELEVISION GUIDE

Watch the children's faces light up when you suggest writing an imaginary television guide.

Materials Needed: pencils and paper

Directions:

Discuss the information and format of a television guide. The children create imaginary television programs and write a brief description of each program.

Fargo *TV Guide*
Grand Forks

FRIDAY
Morning

7:00 1 Soupy Sam—comedy
Soupy Sam gets caught by the police for littering
7 Morning Surprise—Exercise
11 Today—Discussion
7:30 3 Do It Yourself—Learn to sew by hand
4 Use Your Ball—Dodgeball and Soccer games

	5	Cook Yourself—How to make pumpkin pie and pizza
8:00	1	Cartoon Party—Popeye
	7	Leaf-a-Wreath—Make wreaths
	11	Pets—Training your pet dogs
8:30	5	Wear Funny Hair—Show long-haired wigs
	11	Take a Trip—Pretend to go to France
9:00	1	Movie—comedy GoGa the Lion—About a lion who thinks he's smart but he's not (60 minutes)
	7	Know Your Clock—Learn the twelve o'clocks
	5	Knit it yourself—How to knit a hat
9:30	7	Science Glurtch—a kind of formula Pollution
10:00	7	News
10:30	5	Art Project—Painting
11:00	3	Story—Bingo
12:00	1	News

NONSENSE WORDS

A nonsense word stimulates very original stories since the nonsense word itself is original. Children think it's great fun to think up their own nonsense words, too!

Materials Needed: tape recorder for dictacting stories, pencil and paper for writing stories

Directions:

Give each child a nonsense word to write at the top of his paper. The children use the nonsense words to create stories or plays.

Creative Nonsense Stories (Written)

Zilly

Zilly is a Zebra.
She is a laughing Zebra.
She loves to laugh.
She'd rather laugh then eat.
She laughs funny.

Mary, Grade 2

Frippled

Frippled is a kind of chewing gum. It is coconut flavor. It tastes good. But my little sister doesn't like it. One day a boy came to our house and said to his mommy, I'm hungry. ''No you aren't you just had din-

Gramfur

Gramfur is Santa's middle name so it sounds like this, Santa Gramfur Claus, the first. They named him Gramfur because fur is like Santa's beard. The Gram in Gramfur was a game called Gram that Santa played when he went to school. When Santa has a kid he's going to make it like this Santa Gramfur, the Second.

Katy, Grade 5

Quinning

Quinning is a new outfit. It's called the quinning outfit. It has 1 top, 1 pair of pants, 1 skirt, and 1 pair of shorts. The shirt is pink, purple, white, red, blue, orange, yellow, silver, and gold striped. The pants are black. The skirt is brown and the shorts are gray. It's a real groovy outfit. All the dogs are wearing this quinning outfit every day.

Suzy, Grade 6

Falishka

Falishka is a kind of instrument. It is curly and square. A little man made it. He got a box and cut some keys in it. Then he made a hole to blow into. One day one of the keys broke so he put a blue one in. He made songs for it. Here's one. Lalalalalala Hey Hee Hee boo boo ba ba Oh!

Lisa, Grade 3

ner." I am too and he began to cry. So my mom said Sally go get Tommy a piece of Frippled. So Sally ran to her room and took out a piece of gum out of her drawer and brang it to Tommy. Tommy tore off the paper and shoved it into his mouth. Mmm I love it shouted Tommy I love it I love it. You got any more. Sally said Yes but you can't have any. Tommy began to cry.

Sally said, O.K. I'll give you one more piece. She ran to her room and got Tommy another piece of Frippled.

Tommy stuck it in his mouth and said ICK! I hate it, I hate it, I hate it—this Frippled and he spit it out on the carpet.

That night Sally's mom said why did Tommy like his Frippled the first time and not the second. Sally said because I put soap in it. So he wouldn't ask for more.

She began to laugh. The End

Cara, Grade 4

Falishka, the Fish

Once there was a mean fish and he had a wife and her name was Falishka. Mr. fish did not like where he was so then one day Falishka asked to move to the Red River and so they swam to the Red River. But Mr. Fish did not like it there and Falishka said, What do you want? Mr. Fish said for years and years I only wanted a Coke for a fish so she got one for him and they were happy forever.

David, Grade 3

PAPER PLATE STORIES

Paper plates for writing? Why not—it works! Yes, some paper plates are so picturesque and colorful that when a paper plate is brought to school children may correlate writing with the picture or design on the plate.

Materials Needed: paper plates that have a picture or design on them, writing paper, yarn (optional), masking tape (optional)

Preparations:

Ask children to bring used, but clean, figured paper plates to school. Yarn or masking tape can be used for hanging.

Directions:

Students write about the picture or design on the paper plate and then hang their writings near the plate as a wall hanging, mobile, or bulletin board display.

Variation:

For an independent activity, hang a number of different types of plates on the walls. When students feel creative, they may write about one of the plates and then, using masking tape,

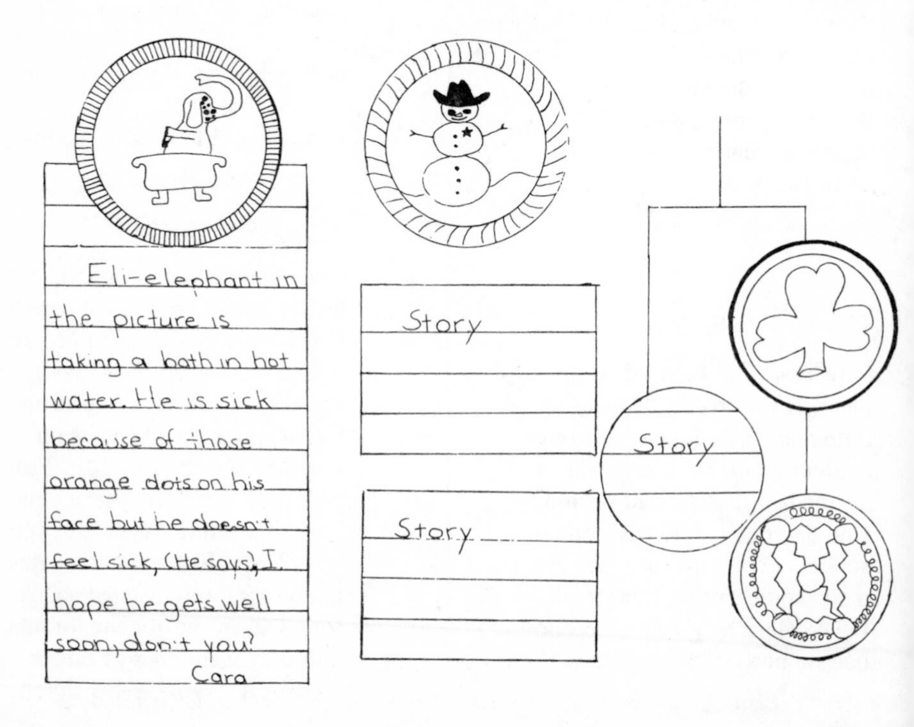

they hang their writing on the wall near the proper plate. The masking tape is even motivating!

PASS THE HAT

Most children are too curious to pass up this activity. Each child draws a picture sticker out of a hat and then writes a story, poem, riddle, or a description relating to the sticker.

Materials Needed: writing paper, a sticker (picture or a word written on a piece of paper), paper plate, pipe cleaner (one long one or two short ones), stapler or glue

Preparation:

1. Make the paper plate hat as seen in illustrations.
2. Put stickers inside hat.

Directions:

Each child draws a sticker from the hat and then writes a story, poem, riddle, or a description relating to the sticker. The sticker may be glued on the writing paper wherever each child wishes. A picture may be drawn on the rest of the paper if only a sentence is written.

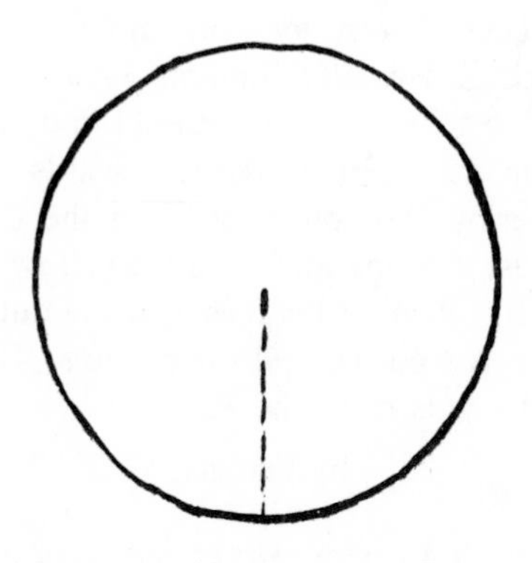

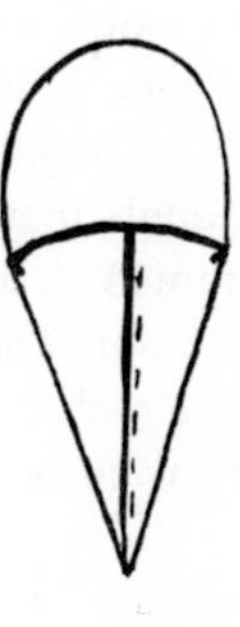

STORIES FROM STORIES

Students can write stories by simply beginning with a word from a familiar story. This activity encourages creative writing while the word that is used often becomes more meaningful to the students. For example, after the story of "Curious George" the word "curious" can be discussed and written on the blackboard for children to use in their writings. Some children may write sentences using the word "curious" while others may write more detailed stories.

Directions:

Teacher (or student) selects a word from a book for creative writing experiences.

I'm curious about candy machines. by Mike, Grade 2

I am curious about my Christmas presents. I am curious about my Birthday presents. by Marcia, Grade 2

I'm more curious then curious George. I am curious about a lots of things. Like snow and stuf like that. And a lots more things. I'm curious, curious, curious! by Jill, Grade 2

"Curious George in the Spooky House"

This is George. He lived with his friend the man with the yellow hat. One day somebody knocked at the door. The man with the yellow hat went to answer it. It was the man from the bakery truck. He had come to give him the peanuts for George's surprise party. Then the man said, "I will be going to town. Would you like to come with me?" he said to George and the man jumped into the truck. They stopped at a spooky house and the man walked out of the car and said, "I'm going to the store across the street. You stay here George." And he walked off. Then George took one more look at the spooky house and he was curious. He had to find out what was in it. So he jumped out of the car to take a look and could you have guessed what happened? George saw a ghost flying towards him although they were sheets covering Balloons. Just then the door slammed. George was scared. Just then the man with the yellow hat came out. Then Nancy, then Billy, then all his friends came out. It was a real surprise party and George got into all the peanuts. Then they went home and has a good nights rest. The End

by Pamela, Grade 2

VARIOUS OTHER DICTATING-WRITING IDEAS

- Place an object in a box (or sack) and pass the box around the classroom. Without looking inside the children describe the object they think is in the box.
- Each child is given a small object such as a watermelon seed to glue on his writing paper and then he writes about that particular object.
- The students write a description of a story character, television

star, or historical figure. Each description is read aloud and the class guesses who is being described.

- The students walk a short distance to a certain place in the community and, after returning to school, write directions to this place. Follow these directions to see if they are correct.
- A child may tell or write directions to a game, then play it.
- A student may tell or write a familiar story with an additional character—himself.
- Place a pair of buttons or plastic eyes and a felt mouth (might use masking tape) on some object in the room. The children pretend these objects come alive and can talk. What do the objects say?
- The children write a list of all the sounds they hear at home, at school, or on a walk.
- The students act as reporters and interview a person at home or at school. With this information, they write a report for the rest of the class.
- Students who design hats may be in a fashion show. Each person writes about his own hat and these essays are read at the fashion show.
- Glue used greeting cards on writing paper and place these cards in the writing center. The children write creative verses and greetings to correlate with the designs.
- A student writes a riddle about something in the room and the rest of the class tries to guess the answer.
- Students write creative stories or poems to read on the tape recorder.
- Keep a poem and/or story file so the children can read each other's writings.
- Write an imaginary recipe and illustrate the finished product.
- The children write mathematical stories that involve solving a problem. Each child then reads his story to a small group who try to solve the problem.
- When putting on a play ask the children to decide which character they would most like to portray and to write their reasons for choosing this particular part.
- Two children imagine that they have very bad colds and have lost their voices. They take turns writing to each other on the blackboard.
- Dictate (on tape if desired) or write:

an invitation
a thank-you note
a letter
an announcement
a newspaper article
a poem, riddle and/or joke
a fable, a tall tale, or any other kind of story
a play or puppet show
about a dream
about an imaginary machine
about an imaginary animal
about a famous person
some Haiku verses
some suggestions for lesson plans and/or ideas for the learning centers

- Sometimes I'm:

responsible	wondering	excited
proud	wishing	pleased
curious	hoping	thankful
afraid	sad	tired
concerned	angry	singing
careful	hurt	sorry
impatient	embarrased	worried
happy	thinking	surprised

WORDS FOR THE MONTH

Words are more meaningful when the children relate them to one central idea. Aspects of the different months unify these word lists.

Materials Needed: writing paper, pencil, construction paper, scissors, a large sheet of construction paper for each envelope (optional)

Directions:

1. Children suggest an appropriate symbol for the month and the words that relate to that month.
2. Teacher prints (or types) these words inside the symbol and supplies a dittoed sheet for each child. (Older children may print the words on their own symbol.)

3. Children may use these words in their creative writing during the month.
4. If desired, each student may cut out and glue this symbol to the outside of a large envelope. The student's stories are kept in this envelope.

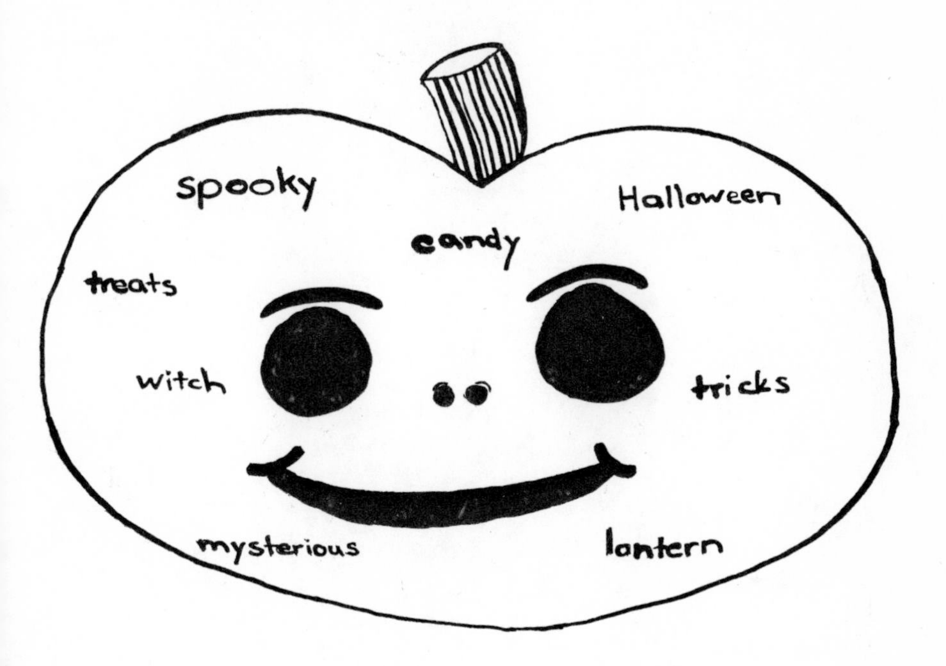

Chapter 3

Performing in the Looking Glass

ACTIVITIES FOR DRAMA

Here are a number of ideas to stimulate your students to participate in drama.

Finish the story:
The teacher or a student begins a story. Then children form small groups to plan an ending to the story. Each group dramatizes how it would end the story.

Pass the hat:
Pictures of animals and people are cut out and placed in a hat. Three or four children draw a picture from the hat and make up a play or puppet show using whatever characters are portrayed in the picture. If a puppet show is desired, the pictures (cards) can be pasted on a Popsicle stick.

Demonstration Day:
Hold a "demonstration day" at school. Everyone may demon-

strate how to do something such as telling time, knitting, playing the piano, how to bat a baseball, etc. Children choose their own demonstration projects, which they can do either alone or with a partner.

Dramatize:

1. the sequence of a newspaper comic strip which is suitable to the children's reading level.
2. a nursery rhyme, poem, or a story as someone reads it.
3. a mathematical story problem. The other students give the answer.
4. a feeling such as a "happy feeling." The rest of the children guess why this person feels that way.
5. being a salesman who is trying to sell a book or some other item.
6. a puppet show in front of a mirror. Then present it to a group, if desired.
7. being a story character, a specific worker, or a famous person. Other class members try to guess who is being portrayed.
8. a superstition and have other children guess what the superstition is. (Children will probably want to research and study about superstitions before they try this activity.)

COSTUMES

Easy Paper Towel Costumes

A child seems to feel more like the character he is portraying when he designs a costume that helps him identify with a specific character. These costumes are so easy to make that a child can make them by himself. Perhaps you will want to keep a roll of paper towels in the drama center for the costume designers who happen along.

Materials Needed: roll of institutional (uncut) paper towels, scissors, crayons, masking tape, yarn or string

Directions:

The child cuts two strips of paper towels and glues them together widthwise. A costume is designed with crayons. In the center of the costume, two slots are cut, one each way, so the head will slip through. The inside of the costume is reinforced

with masking tape at the end of each slot. Yarn or string tied around the waist makes a belt.

Interfacing Costumes

Interfacing, a fabric that can be bought in most variety or fabric stores, is so easy to cut and color that even the youngest students can make this kind of costume. If washable crayons are used on interfacing costumes, most of the color will wash out and the costumes can be reused again and again.

Materials Needed: interfacing fabric, washable crayons, scissors, yarn or string, paper punch (optional)

Preparations:

1. Cut a rectangle from a piece of fabric large enough to cover both front and back of a child.
2. In the center of the piece of fabric, cut two small slots, one each way so that the child's head can slip through.
3. Use yarn for a belt or punch holes in each side of garment and tie each side together with yarn.

Directions:

The children decorate the costumes with washable crayons.

Costumes can be washed, dried (hand or machine), and redesigned with washable crayons.

Variations:

1. Scarves, belts, ribbons, hankies: cut out desired shapes, design with washable crayons, wash and redesign.

Transparent Lid Masks

Sometimes it is easier for children, especially the shy ones, to participate in dramatizations if they use a mask. Hand masks can be made from large transparent lids that allow the child to see out easily and to move about safely. These plastic masks can be designed over and over again because the crayon is easily rubbed off.

Materials Needed: canned ham lids or large coffee can lids, crayons, yarn (optical)

Directions:

With crayons, yarn, etc., each child decorates a lid to hold in front of his face. If the lids are to be tied on, a hole should be cut out for the mouth and nose so that the child can breathe easily. The crayon designs will rub off; therefore, these masks can be designed as often as desired.

Variation:

These lids can also be used for puppets. If a waxed paper roll is glued to the lid, it will serve as a handle.

Wigs and Toupees

Children enjoy wearing wigs and toupees when they're participating in role play, creative dramatics, or when they're portraying a specific character from a story or play. These wigs and toupees are time-consuming, so you might suggest to the children that they work with partners or organize an assembly line when they make them. This activity may help develop the younger students' tying skills. Bows can be tied to represent curly hair, if desired.

Materials Needed: fruit or vegetable plastic net sacks, yarn or cord, scissors

Preparations:

1. Cut widthwise across the sack (leaving about 8 inches for the wig).
2. Weave yarn in and out of the holes. At the top, pull tight, and tie to make a cap shape.

Directions:

The child cuts a piece of yarn, laces it through a section of net, and then knots it. This process is continued until the desired amount of hair (yarn) is attached. Hairpieces and toupees are made in the same way, except that the net is cut smaller and the yarn is cut shorter.

PLAYS

Children's Plays

A magazine of student's plays, which is sent home to be shared with the family, helps encourage the children to write plays for a purpose and permits the family to enjoy the delightful imaginations and talents of the children. When a letter is sent home with the magazine, it helps parents to understand the importance and accomplishment of writing and directing a play.

Materials Needed: writing paper, pencils, ditto paper, stapler, and construction paper for the magazine covers

Preparation:

1. Ditto (or print on a chart) a simple form for a play (use the form as in the plays that follow if you wish).
2. Type and ditto the play so that each character can have a script for his own use. Save each ditto master to use for making the magazine at a later date.
3. Write a letter to parents, or simply modify the following one to send home with the Children's Plays.

Dear Parents,

The children have written so many delightful plays that we would like to share some of them with you through our Children's Plays magazine. Each child (sometimes with a partner) planned, organized, wrote, read to the teacher, and directed his own play. The playwright chose puppets or some other children to be the characters in his play.

We hope that you will enjoy the plays as much as we have enjoyed them.

Sincerely,

Directions:

The children might read, as well as participate in, a number of plays (use plays that follow if you desire) before they attempt to write a play. After a child writes and directs a play, alone or with a partner, it may be accepted for publication in Children's Plays. After the plays are written, dittoed, and stapled into a booklet, the students can decorate their own cover before they take it home to share with their family. Keep a play booklet in the drama center so children can read and dramatize them whenever they wish.

The following plays were written by second graders:

Summer Time by Perry and Darin

Dick:
Sally:
Harry:
Dad:
Mom:
Beth:

Scene 1

Mom: Time to wake up, kids.
Beth: O.K.
Dick: Dad will you fix my bike?
Dad: O.K. Dick. (They go in the yard.)
Mom: I'm going to clean up.

Scene 2

Sally: I'll help you Mom.
Mom: O.K. Sally.
Dad: Dick, mow the lawn.
Dick: O.K. Daddy.
Harry: Dad what can I do?
Dad: You can help Dick mow the lawn.
Harry: O.K. Daddy.

(Harry and Dick mow the lawn)

The Party by Jill

Mini Mutt.
Kitty Cat:
Sammy Squirrel:
Chirpy Chipmunk:
Spanky Sparrow:

Chirpy: Where are all my friends today?
(Animals behind Chirpy)
Mini: Won't Chirpy be surprised when we give him the party this afternoon?
Spanky: Yes. I have the balloons.
Kitty: I got the cake.
Sammy: I have the Koolade.
Chirpy: Where is everybody anyway?
(All animals) Surprise! Surprise!
Spanky: It's a party for you because you're such a good friend.
Chirpy: Well thank-you, thank-you, thank-you very much!
Mini: Let's serve the cake and put up the balloons.
Kitty: Let's go play in the forest and have some more fun.

Guide for Mother Goose Play

Children love to become playwrights and performers by writing and presenting their own plays. The following suggestions can help a teacher guide her students in creating an easy Mother Goose Play with minimal preparations and practices. Remember to keep it simple!

Materials Needed: simple props and costumes should be available, if needed

Preparation:

Teach nursery rhyme songs before a play

Directions:

The teacher might start this activity by telling the children that they may become actors and actresses by writing a play and presenting it to another class or to their parents. The words, "playwright," "actor," "actress," "prop," "role," "stage" might be discussed at this time. The teacher might suggest an idea for the play: "Boys and girls, maybe we can give Mother Goose a party in the play that we write. What kind of party would you like to give her?" Use whatever kind of party that the children suggest. The children select the nursery rhyme characters that they wish to portray, and the costumes and props may be brought from home or made in the art center. For example, Jack-Be-Nimble can carry a candle in a clay candle holder.

"A Happy Day for Mother Goose"

CHILDREN: (sing) "Happy Birthday" or "Happy Mother's Day"

(depending on the kind of party it is).

MOTHER GOOSE: What a nice surprise! Everyone must be here—a parade of Mother Goose friends!

(Children in turn walk to front of stage to sing or say their rhymes. The rhymes which the children choose might include some of the following:)

"Jack-Be-Nimble" (candle placed in holder)
"Rub-A-Dub-Dub" (tub from paper)
"Polly Put the Kettle On" (kettle for Polly)
"Ride a Cock-Horse" (galloping music can be played as children gallop around the room on stick horses)
"The Three Little Kittens" (mittens)
"Little Jumping Joan" (all count while Joan jumps rope)
"To Market, To Market" (basket)
"See-Saw" (see-saw rhythms)
"Queen of Hearts" (tray of hearts and a crown on queen)
"Please Porridge Hot" (action to verse)

MOTHER GOOSE: Thank you for everything. You've made me so happy!

CHILDREN: You've always told us, Mother Goose, that a good way to be happy is to make others happy.

SONG: "Good Night, Mother Goose" (Tune to "Good Night, Ladies")

Through the Year

The following program is a pleasant way to summarize the events of the school year (or midterm). An informal program enables each student to plan, organize, and demonstrate to his parents (or another class) some of the skills acquired throughout the school year.

Materials Needed: save a variety of the children's work such as art and craft projects, scrapbooks, recycled inventions, science experiments, etc., or have them bring their handiwork from home. These materials can be used for a table and a bulletin board display entitled, "Through the Year."

Directions:

The class handles all the arrangements for the program. First they discuss, month by month, the activities that took place during the year. Each student thinks of a program activity to do alone (or with a small group) such as jumping rope, participating in an original play, presenting a musical number, displaying an individual art show, etc. (This is an excellent time to informally introduce or reinforce such words as "solo," "duet," "trio," and "quartet.") The children send invitations to parents, set up the table and bulletin board displays, plan simple refreshments (optional), and practice a few times in front of the other students.

Directly before the performance each child acts as a host or hostess and shows parents to their chairs. Directly after the performance the parents are given refreshments.

PROPERTIES

Box Buildings

When you discover how easy these buildings are to make and how much the children enjoy them, you will probably have them in your room more often. Box buildings are fun to use in dramatizations and they are ideal for studying about homes and occupations. In fact, sometime you might find a whole community in your room—fire station, bakery, hardware store, grocery store, etc.

Materials Needed: large grocery boxes, paint and brushes, small stick

Preparations:

1. Cut down (from top to bottom) the center of one of the widest sides of the box and along the bottom of this side. (This is the back of the building.)
2. Fold three flaps down into the box (or cut them off), leaving the front flap up to represent the top part of the house.
3. Cut off the two top corners of this front flap and glue a

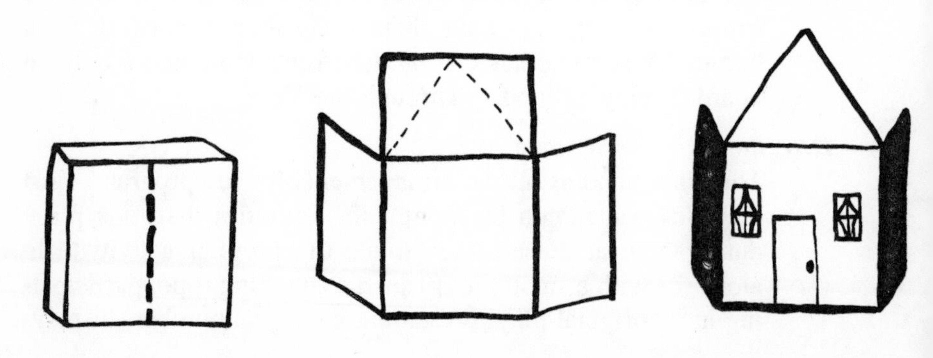

stick on the back of this flap (inside house) to hold it in place. See illustration that follows.

Directions:

Paint box buildings as needed for role play, dramatizations, social studies activity, and/or for any time there is a use for a building. When buildings are not in use they can become temporary room dividers.

Roll-Up Puppet Theater

A long roll of corregated paper makes a handy puppet theater to use in a classroom (especially a classroom with limited space) since it can be rolled up and easily stored whenever it is not in use.

Materials Needed: a long roll of corregated paper, clothespins, scissors (optional)

Preparations:

Cut a stage window in the middle at the top of the corregated roll (or leave it plain so children can sit on chairs and manipulate their puppets over the top of the theater).

Directions:

The children can set up the theater by unrolling it whenever they need it. Roll each end into a pole and attach clothespins on the poles to keep them from unrolling.

PUPPETS

Card Puppets

Children love to recycle used greeting cards, playing cards, and valentines into stick puppets to use for their original puppet shows.

Materials Needed: suitable greeting cards, playing cards, and/or valentines, Popsicle sticks, glue

Directions:

The children cut animals and other suitable characters and objects from cards and glue them on Popsicle sticks.

Variation:

Glue cards on writing paper and then write a verse or story about the character or object from the card.

Color-on-Puppet

These color-on-puppets can supply many hours of creative art and language experiences for children. The paper towel puppets are so easy to make that if cardboard puppet patterns and a roll of paper towels are available in the drama center, children can make the puppets by themselves during their spare time.

Materials Needed: paper towels, cardboard, puppet pattern (on page 65), scissors, glue, crayons or marking pens, paper clips or pins (optional)

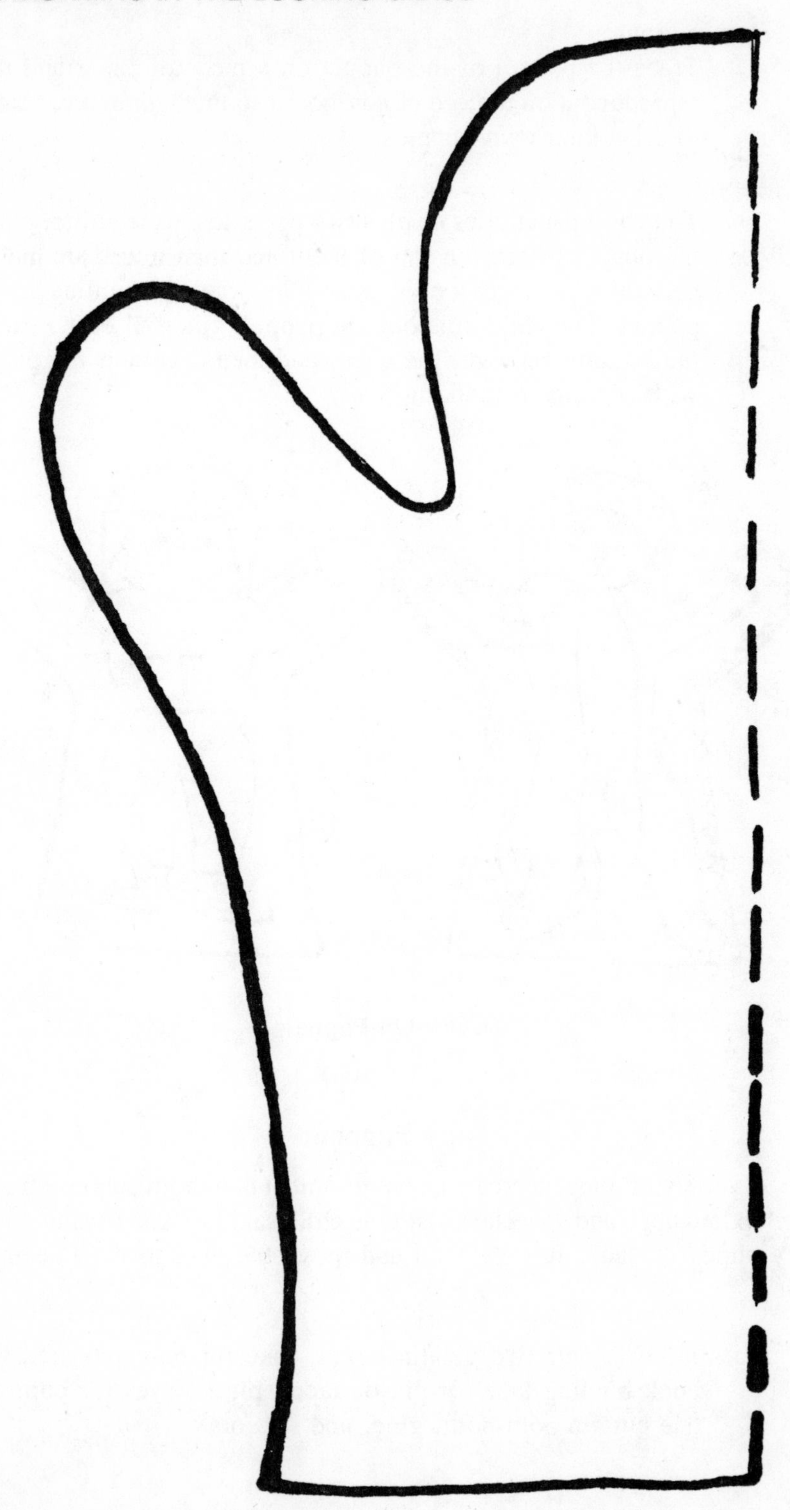

Preparations:

Trace the pattern of the puppet on a piece of paper and then reproduce it on a piece of cardboard so that children can use it to draw their own puppets.

Directions:

The child paper clips or pins two paper towels together, places the puppet pattern on top of them and then traces around the pattern with a crayon or pencil to draw the outline of the puppet. The child cuts out the puppet, glues all edges except the bottom, removes the clips, and then decorates the puppet with crayons or marking pens.

Color-On-Puppets

Furry Puppets

A variety of puppets create an environment that motivates children to develop language and speech skills. One child said he liked to play with a furry puppet because its soft head and moveable eyes made it seem so alive.

Materials Needed: two gelatin boxes, fake fur remnants, red felt, book binding tape (or plastic tape), plastic eyes (or buttons), one curtain pom-pom, glue, and scissors

Preparations:

1. Glue red felt on one side of each gelatin box to represent the mouth.
2. Cover the rest of the box with fake fur.
3. Attach boxes together with tape as seen in the illustration thai follows.
4. Now glue on pom-pom nose, plastic eyes, and furry ears.
5. Place puppets in the learning centers so they are available for the children.

Variation:

1. Older students can make their own puppets.
2. Puppets can be made with Contact paper instead of fur.

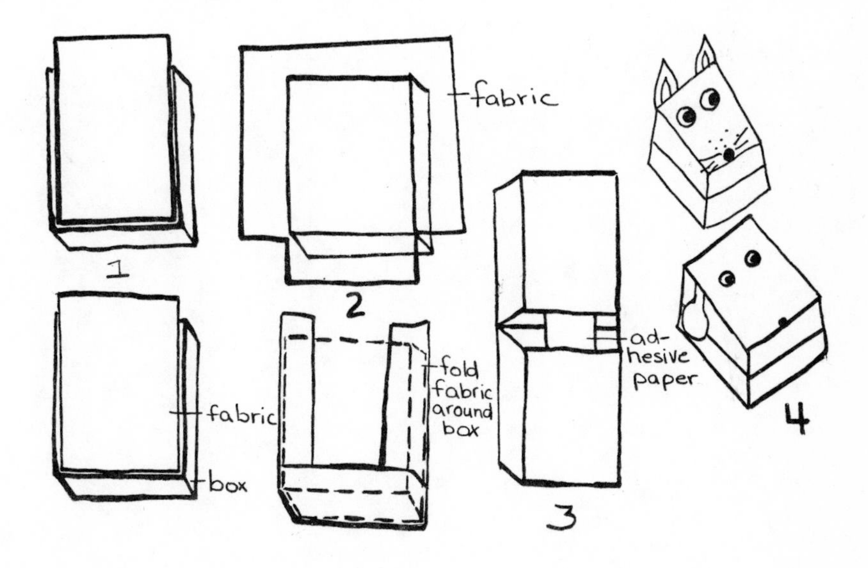

Chapter 4

Felt Board Activities That Teach

COMIC STRIP PUZZLES

Here's an excellent way to use newspaper comic strips in the classroom. These puzzles encourage children to read the comics and to concentrate on the sequence of events that take place in them.

Materials Needed: felt board, felt pieces or sandpaper, comic strips from newspaper, scissors, envelope (or boxes) to hold puzzles

Preparations:

1. Cut out each section of a comic strip.
2. Glue a small piece of felt to the back of each section.
3. Store in an envelope or box that is kept near the felt board.

Directions:

The children arrange the various comic puzzles into the proper sequence on the felt board. If an extra copy of the comic strip that a child is using can be made available, the child may check his own sequence.

Variations:

The children may arrange these puzzles on a table instead of a felt board.

COMPOSERS

A felt board designed to represent a musical staff allows a child to experiment with music and to compose a simple tune that can be played on an instrument.

Materials Needed: felt, yarn, felt board, musical instrument

Preparation:

Make a musical staff on the felt board, using felt for the notes and yarn for the lines of the staff.

Directions:

A child arranges felt notes on the musical staff to compose a tune for someone to play on a piano, tonette, xylophone, or other suitable instrument. The child may wish to write some lyrics to go with the tune.

Variation:

The notes might be seasonal such as pumpkins, bells, or valentine notes.

FELT BOARD ENVELOPE

Clasp envelopes are turned into individual felt boards to create a learning aid that can be applied to many diversified reading and mathematic activities. It is an excellent way to recycle envelopes as well! The envelopes serve as both felt board and storage for felt pieces.

Materials Needed: clasp mailing envelopes (approximately 9″ × 12″), felt, glue, scissors, tagboard

Preparation:

1. Glue a piece of felt to the front of an envelope.
2. Cut a variety of numerals and symbols from felt and place them inside the envelope. Letters and words can be written on tagboard and backed with felt or sandpaper.

Directions:

A student can use the felt items by placing them on his felt envelope when he studies about:

matching shapes
classifications
equations
measurement
geometry
fractions
sequence puzzles
original stories
contractions
compound words
prefixes and suffixes
phonetic skills
games

Variation:

See "Felt Board Math Stories" in this section.

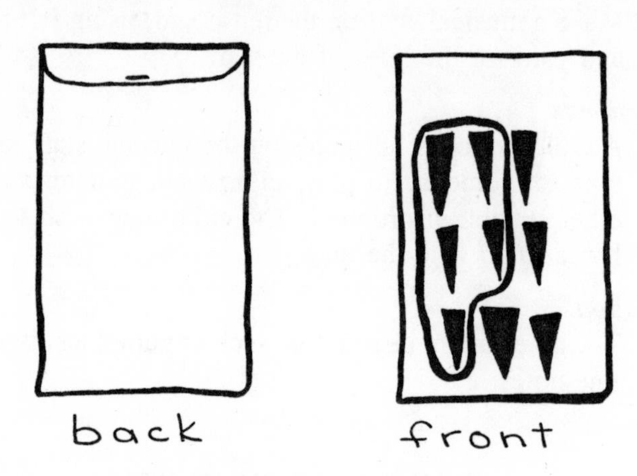

FELT BOARD MATH STORIES

Some children like to solve math stories by using visual and manipulative symbols on a felt board. Here are examples of a variety of math stories which involve either a small or a large felt board.

Materials Needed: felt board (see felt envelope in this chapter), felt symbols, math story sheets, scissors

Preparation:

1. Write and ditto math stories.
2. Cut appropriate symbols from felt (or cut paper symbols and back with felt.)

Directions:

Children read and solve math stories by using the appropriate symbols on the felt board. The answers can be written directly on the dittoed math sheet or on a plastic covered math sheet.

1. Make a large ring with the yarn. Put two blue circles inside the ring. Now put two red circles inside the ring. How many circles are inside the ring? ______
2. Place nine squares inside the ring. Now take three of these squares and place them outside the ring. How many squares are left inside the ring? ______
3. Put six triangles on the felt board. Take one-half (½) of the triangles off the board. How many triangles are left on the

board?_____How many triangles did you remove from the board? ______

4. Put five squares inside the blue ring and four inside the yellow ring. Which color ring holds the most squares?____ Which ring holds the least? ______
5. Place side by side on the board a two inch strip and a nine inch strip of yarn. How much longer is the nine inch piece of yarn than the two inch piece of yarn? ______

FELT-MAGNETIC BOARD

Another type of individualized learning aid that is similar to the felt envelope is the felt-magnetic board made out of a stove pad. These boards are particularly valuable because they involve both visual and manipulative activities. They are also sturdy and portable, and a greater variety of items can be used with them.

Materials Needed: stove pad (available at most variety stores), felt, magnetic tape or small magnets, interfacing, construction paper, box, scissors, glue

Various materials that will adhere to felt boards are: flannel, yarn, foam, sponges, styrofoam, felt, pipe cleaners, sandpaper and some fabrics, such as terry cloth, interfacing, and fake fur.

Preparation:

1. Glue felt on the asbestos side of stove pad.
2. Cut interfacing or felt into symbols, letters, numerals, etc. for use on the felt board.
3. Cut construction paper into desired letters, symbols, etc. and glue magnetic tape on back for use on the metal side.
4. A box can be used to store items for boards.

Directions:

Each child may use his felt-magnetic board for placing pictures or symbols in sequence, displaying illustrations of original stories, studying equations, matching words or symbols, spelling, etc.

GINGERBREAD MEN

Ten to twelve gingerbread men make excellent visual and manipulative aids for mathematics, dramatizations, creative stories, and games.

Materials Needed: felt, scissors, cardboard, glue and felt board

Preparation:

1. Make a gingerbread man pattern from cardboard.
2. Trace gingerbread men on felt and cut them out.
3. Glue felt circles (buttons) on each gingerbread man—one circle on one man, two circles on another man, etc.
4. Glue a felt numeral on the back of each gingerbread man to correspond with the number of buttons on the front.

Directions:

The children place the gingerbread men in sequence on a felt board. Concepts such as "before," "after," "between," "greater," "less," "most" may be reinforced by using these gingerbread men in simple games.

STORY—"KARLA'S BIG DECISION"

The children become directly involved in this felt board story by participating at designated intervals. The balloons reinforce concepts of colors and the words that represent them. The story may also serve as a way to introduce creative storytelling with the felt board.

Materials Needed: felt board, tracing paper, clown pattern at the end of this section, paper (or interfacing fabric) for clown, felt or sandpaper for backing clown

Preparations:

1. Trace clown pattern and cut paper balloons from construction paper.
2. Glue felt or sandpaper to the back of the clown and the balloons so they will adhere to the felt board.
3. Become familiar with the story so that it will be easy to tell (or read) while manipulating objects on the felt board.

Directions:

The children sit in front of the felt board while the teacher tells the story. When the teacher gives a designated gesture, the children participate in the story.

Variations:

1. Dramatize the story.
2. Illustrate the part of the story children like best.

Karla's Big Decision

(A Child Participation Story)

Karla walked slowly down the front steps of her house. Her right hand was tightly closed around a small object and every now and then she stopped to peek inside her fist. Her friend Tom saw her through the window of his house next door, and called out, "Hey, Karla! What's in your hand?" Tom raced outside to see what Karla was holding.

"See! I just earned a quarter this morning. I helped Dad pull weeds in our garden."

"What are you going to buy?"

"Oh, I don't know," said Karla. "I'm going down town to look around. Maybe I'll see something today or maybe I'll wait till some other day."

"I'll go with you," said Tom, "in case you decide."

Together Karla and Tom skipped down the sidewalk towards town, talking of all the things that could be bought for a quarter or less—whistles and comics, candy and gum, balls and other toys.

"Oh! look at all those balloons above the trees. They look like bubbles in the air," Karla said.

"I'll bet Balloon-O is selling balloons again today," said Tom.

"Who's Balloon-O?"

"You know Balloon-O. He's the clown who sells balloons outside the toystore. The balloons are filled with helium gas so they go way up in the air. They're really neat and they only cost a quarter apiece."

"Well, let's go see Balloon-O. Maybe I'll buy a balloon from him."

"Great idea," said Tom skipping a little faster to keep in step with Karla.

Soon they passed Jay and David who were playing a game of tag in their front yard.

"Where are you going and can we go with you?" called Jay.

"Sure, come on," said Tom.

Karla led the children in single file down the sidewalk; she pretended that she was galloping on a pony and she sang a song to the tune of "Here We Go Round the Mulberry Bush." (sing or read)

"We're going down town to see the clown,
To see the clown, to see the clown.
We're going down town to see the clown,
Galloping on our ponies."

In the next block Karla saw some friends playing ball, and she beckoned them to join her, so Beth, Kim, Randy, and Bruce hurried to the end of the line and sang with them as they all galloped along:

"We're going down town to see the clown,
To see the clown, to see the clown.
We're going down town to see the clown,
Galloping on our ponies."

When they were about a block away from the toystore, they could see many colorful balloons floating in the sky, high above the people, the trees, and the tallest buildings.

"Look," said Tom. "There are six green balloons, four red balloons, two white balloons . . . five blue ones, three orange, and more purple, yellow, and brown ones than I can count."

"And I see Balloon-O," said Karla. "The balloons in his hand look like a big bouquet of flowers."

"Which color do you like best?" asked Tom.

"I don't know . . . I like them all . . . I don't know which one to pick."

"Do you want a yellow balloon?" said Tom.

"Yes, take a yellow balloon," urged the children. (Audience may participate after each color is introduced.)

"Do you want a red balloon?" said Tom.

"Yes, take a red balloon."

"Do you want a brown balloon?"

"Yes, take a brown balloon."

"Do you want a blue balloon?"

"Yes, take a blue balloon."

"Do you want an orange balloon?"

"Yes, take an orange balloon."

''Do you want a white balloon?''

''Yes, take a white balloon.''

''Do you want a purple balloon?''

''Yes, take a purple balloon.''

''Do you want a green balloon?''

''Yes, take a green balloon.''

''Which one *are* you going to pick?'' asked Tom.

''I don't know. I just can't decide,'' said Karla.

''Are you going to buy *any* balloon?'' said the clown.

''No!'' said Karla. ''No, I don't want any.''

''YOU DON'T WANT ANY BALLOON?'' shouted the children all together.

''I can't decide which color I want so I just won't buy any of them.''

Karla stood there silently staring at the balloons. All her friends, except Tom, slowly walked away with disappointed looks.

Suddenly Karla's face brightened and she cried, ''I'll take that one in the center, please!''

''Be with you in a few minutes,'' said the clown, waiting on the customers who had come before her.

''Hey kids, come on back,'' called Tom. ''Karla's buying a balloon after all.''

''Which color did you pick?'' asked the children.

''You have to guess,'' said Karla.

''Yellow.'' (Audience may guess colors.)

''Red.''

''Blue.''

''Brown.''

''Purple.''

''White.''

''Orange.''

''Green.''

All the other customers were gone and the clown turned to Karla. ''Now may I help you?'' he asked.

''Yes!'' Karla handed the clown her quarter and said, ''I want that one in the center.''

''Who guessed the right color?'' asked Tom.

''You all win!'' shouted Karla as she quickly pulled the balloon from the center of the bouquet. ''See! I picked a balloon that has every different color in it!''

All of them clapped as they watched a many-colored balloon appear before them.

''You made a good decision,'' said Balloon-O.

''Thank you! I think I made a good decision, too, don't you?'' Karla said to her newly purchased toy. Then Karla let her many-colored balloon fly as high as the string would stretch as she ran with her friends to play in the park.

VARIOUS OTHER FELT BOARD IDEAS

1. Glue felt, flannel, or sandpaper on the back of pictures from magazines or old books to use with original felt board stories.
2. Partners may work together on matching upper case letters (or words) to lower case letters (or words).

3. Students may be asked to place a sequence of letters, numerals, or pictures on the board in the proper order.
4. Make a toy shelf on the board out of yarn, and define what objects belong on that shelf. Students place toys (made from paper and backed with felt) on a designated shelf. For example, the toys that begin with "d" might belong on the top shelf while those that begin with "b" belong on the bottom.
5. Create out of yarn a simple fruit basket and a simple vegetable basket on the board. Children place the pictures of fruits and vegetables in the proper baskets. (Managers of the produce departments in grocery stores often have extra pictures of fruits and vegetables which they will give teachers upon request.)
6. Students can use boards to study classification, compound words, contractions, initial consonants, final consonants, digraphs, blends, diphthongs, and syllabication.
7. Divide board in half with a piece of yarn. Ask the children to place specific objects on the left and specific objects on the right of the yarn.
8. Students may be asked to divide the board in half, fourths, thirds, etc. with yarn. A felt circle cut in sections may also be used for fractions.

Chapter 5

Games for Fun and Learning

ANIMAL HUNT

Many children are excited by the prospect of hunting for a specified number of animals to put in an imaginary zoo. This game is an excellent way for a zookeeper (teacher) to check on each child's ability to match a numeral on one card with the corresponding number of animals on another card.

Materials Needed: a set of light green cards and a set of yellow cards cut into approximately four × four inch squares (colors may be changed). There should be at least two cards (from each set) for every player.

Preparation:

1. Picture Cards—Draw a different number of animals on each card of one set (or glue animal stickers on cards).
2. Numeral Cards—Write the numeral that corresponds to each picture.

Directions:

The teacher hides the picture cards around the room while the players cover their eyes or stand outside the room. The numeral cards are placed face down in a pile on a table. The zookeeper (teacher) explains that animals are needed for the zoo. Each player selects a numeral card, and then searches for the picture card that has the same number of animals. When a player finds his animals for the zoo, he takes the two cards to the zookeeper. If the cards correspond, (for example, a picture of four bears on one card and the symbol "4" on the other card) he may draw another numeral card and proceed as before. If his cards do not correspond, then he returns his picture to the same hiding place and tries again to find the correct set of animals. The game is over when all of the correct sets of animals are brought to the zookeeper.

Variations:

This game can easily be modified into other games by using other types of matching such as 3-three, dog-log, $3 + 5 = 8$, see-sea, black-white, etc., with each variation placed in an appropriate setting.

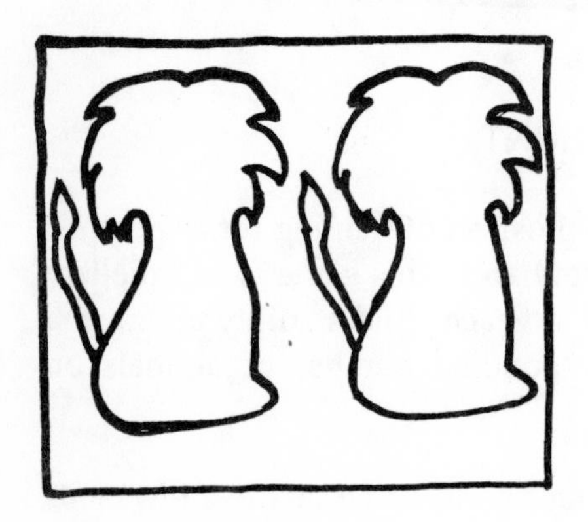

BLOCK GAMES

It is surprising how many different ways counting blocks can be used in the classroom. Construction, Blocky Consonants, Building, and Toss-a-Fact are only a few of the many games that can be played with blocks. Once these games are introduced, children may be encouraged to play them during their spare time.

Construction

Materials Needed: colored counting cubes or other small blocks, self-checking "block cards," trucks to haul blocks (optional).

Preparation:

Make self-checking cards by drawing around blocks on tagboard and coloring them the same colors as the blocks.

Directions:

Some children pretend to be carpenters while the other children act as truck drivers. A carpenter holds up a "block card" which shows the number and color of blocks that the carpenter needs for his construction project. The truck driver attempts to transport the correct number as well as the correct color of blocks to the carpenter. The carpenter and driver lay the blocks on the "block card" to check to see that the truck driver brought the correct color and number of blocks to the carpenter. If not, the driver attempts to correct the order.

Variation: For additional experiences, students may use play money to buy each block.

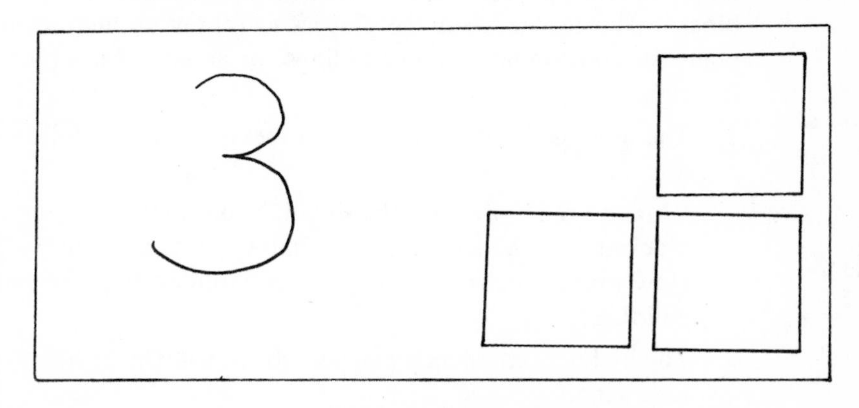

Blocky Consonants

Materials Needed: one counting cube (or small block) for each player, a piece of paper, marking pen, score sheet (optional)

Preparation:

Print a different consonant on each side of a block. Make a block for each player.

Directions:

Two to six players sit around a table (or on the floor). A piece of paper is placed in the center of the table, approximately the same distance from each player. The teacher (or student) says a word which begins with one of the consonants on the blocks. Each player looks on his block for the initial consonant of the pronounced word ("top"—"t"). When he finds the block he places it on the paper with the correct initial consonant facing the top. The first player who places his block correctly on the paper earns a point. The player who has the most points at a given length of time wins the game.

Variation: This game can easily be modified to develop vowels, blends, and digraphs by simply changing the letters on the blocks.

Building

(Building Math Vocabulary and Math Concepts with Blocks)

Materials Needed: a container of colored blocks

Directions:

Place the container of blocks in the center of a table (or on the floor). A small group of players gather around the container of blocks. The teacher asks the players to follow an architect's plans for constructing some buildings, or an engineer's plans for highways:

1. The architect's plans might be something like the following:

   "Make a red building 2 blocks tall. Make a blue building 3 blocks tall." Which building is tallest? Which is shortest? How many blocks taller is the blue building than the red building?

2. The highway engineer's plans might be something like the following:

   "Build the Red Highway 2 blocks wide and 6 blocks long. Build the Blue Highway 4 blocks wide and 6 blocks long." Compare these highways in length and width. Who will tell us about the comparisons you have made?

Variations: "Building" stories can easily be adapted to various levels of learning. "Building" vocabulary can include:

few, fewer, fewest
short, shorter, shortest
high, higher, highest
tall, taller, tallest
narrow, narrower, narrowest
wide, wider, widest
long, longer, longest
equal, same amount

Toss-A-Fact

Materials Needed: two counting cubes (or small blocks) for each small group—two or three players and one score keeper, marking pen, score paper, and pencil (optional)

Preparation:

Write a numeral on each side of the two cubes (or masking tape can easily be put on each cube and the numerals can be written on it).

Directions:

The first player shakes the two cubes and drops them lightly on the table (or floor). The players add the two numbers that face the top. (In subtraction the players subtract the smallest from the largest number and in division the largest number is divided by the smallest number.) The player who says the correct answer first receives a point. The game continues for a specified number of points.

CONTRACTION PUZZLES

These contraction puzzles can be placed in a learning center for an independent learning and self-checking activity, or else use them with a group of students in a teacher-directed game to help strengthen the concept of contractions.

Materials Needed: oaktag or construction paper, marking pen or crayons, scissors, container for puzzles

Preparation:

1. Cut (zig-zag) a rectangle in half to make a puzzle.
2. Print a contraction on one half of the rectangle and print the two words the contraction represents on the other half.
3. Make enough puzzles for each person to have one piece.

Directions:

Each person draws a piece of puzzle from a box. After the puzzle pieces are distributed, each person looks for his "partner" (one who holds the corresponding piece of puzzle). The "partners" create and write sentences using their contraction in each sentence. If desired, "partners" may read their sentences aloud to the class.

Variations:

Use this puzzle approach for developing reading skills.

GIVE YOUR DOG A BONE

Sometimes children enjoy making their own games to be played in the classrooms, such as "Give Your Dog A Bone." This is a very flexible game in that different skills can be studied by merely changing the information on the bones.

Materials Needed: tagboard (or lightweight cardboard), bottom (or top) of a box such as a two pound cheese box, scissors, glue, crayons

Preparation:

1. Make your own patterns of a dog and bone from the patterns on the following page. The children can use them to trace their own copies.
2. Prepare a ditto master with an equation printed inside each bone-shaped outline. Later, print the answer on back of each bone making sure that the answer doesn't show on the front of it. (The children might help print the answers on the bones if the teacher checks to see that they are correct.)

Directions for Making Dog:

The children trace around the dog pattern and then cut out the form and color it. Glue the front of the dog to one end of the box and the back of the dog to the opposite end of the box. Cut out the bones and store inside the dog

Give Your Dog A Bone Pattern—Front of Dog

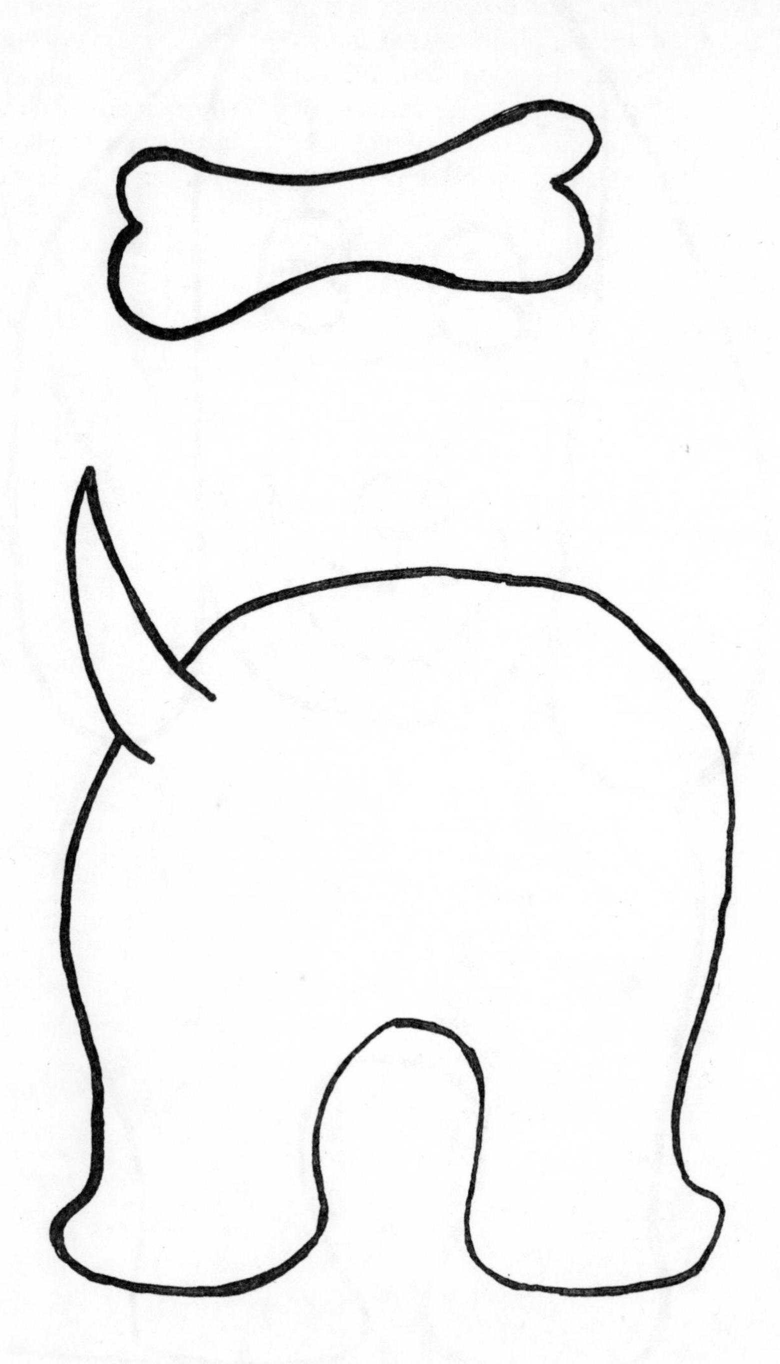

Dog Pattern—Back and Bone

Directions for "Give Your Dog A Bone" Game:

Each player places his dog in front of him. The desired number of bones are placed in a pile with the answer side face down and the question side face up. The first player reads the question from the bone on top of the pile and attempts to answer it. He then picks the bone up to show his opponents the answer. If his answer is correct he gives his dog a bone by sticking the bone through the dog's mouth. If his answer is incorrect he places the bone on a bone pile. The game continues until the bones are gone. The dog who eats the most bones is the winner.

JACK-IN-THE-BOX GAME

Jack-in-the-Box is an easy and inexpensive game that you can make from small milk cartons to stress a variety of basic reading skills. A child can play alone or with a friend.

Materials Needed: cardboard or tagboard, milk carton, colored construction paper or wallpaper, glue, scissors, crayons or marking pens, paper for word cards

Preparation:

1. Decorate milk carton with wallpaper or lightweight construction paper.
2. Trace the pattern of Jack on the following page and transfer it to a piece of tagboard.
3. Color, cut out, and glue Jack inside and to the back of a milk carton.
4. Make word cards that are suitable for the specific skill you wish to stress.
5. An answer key can be made if you desire.

Game 1. Place only words that begin like Jack in his box.

Game 2. Place words that end like Jack in his box.

Game 3. Place words that rhyme with Jack in his box.

Game 4. Create a variety of other characters and give them each a name to use with other games.

Variation:

Use this game with math by having the answer clipped to the

Jack-in-the-Box-Pattern

hat. For example, only the 3+2 2+3 4+1 6−1 cards belong in the box with the boy who has "5" on his hat.

SPELLING GAMES

The following games add fun and interest in developing spelling skills:

Blackboard Game

Materials Needed: blackboard, chalk, tagboard, pictures from magazines or workbooks, a box to hold the picture cards

Preparation:

1. Cut appropriate pictures from books and magazines and paste each of them on a three × three inch piece of tagboard.
2. Write the word that describes the picture on the opposite side of each card.
3. Laminate the cards (optional).
4. Place the cards in a box, picture side up, by the blackboard.

Directions:

At children's discretion, they may go to the blackboard station, look at the picture, and attempt to write the word that represents the picture on the blackboard. The player then turns over his card to check his answer. If the word on the board is spelled like the one on the card, he earns a point. If desired, each time a student plays this game, he tries to improve his score. He wins the game when he has spelled all of the words correctly. Students on a similar spelling level may wish to compete and keep a running score in this game.

Draw and Spell

Materials Needed: pizza plate (or plastic coffee lid), cardboard, pencil and paper, brass fastener

Preparation:

1. Print each letter of the alphabet near the edge of a pizza plate.
2. Make a pointer for the spinner from a piece of cardboard (or plastic lid) and fasten it to the pizza plate with a brass fastener.

Directions:

Each player takes a plain sheet of paper and draws an outline of an object, such as a flower, on it. Inside of the object he draws enough dotted lines for the letters that spell the words that name each part of the flower. (See illustration.) The words that are to spell the various parts of the flower can be written at the top of each player's paper, if desired.

The first player spins the spinner, and, if the point lands on a letter which belongs on one of the dotted lines, he may print it on the proper place (or places) on the line. The letters do not need to come in order. The first player who spells all the words on the flower says "Flower" (or whatever object it happens to be) and he is the winner of the "Draw and Spell" game.

Variation:

Dittoes for this game may be prepared and placed in learning centers so children can play this game at their discretion.

Listen and Spell

Materials Needed: tape recorder, animal sounds

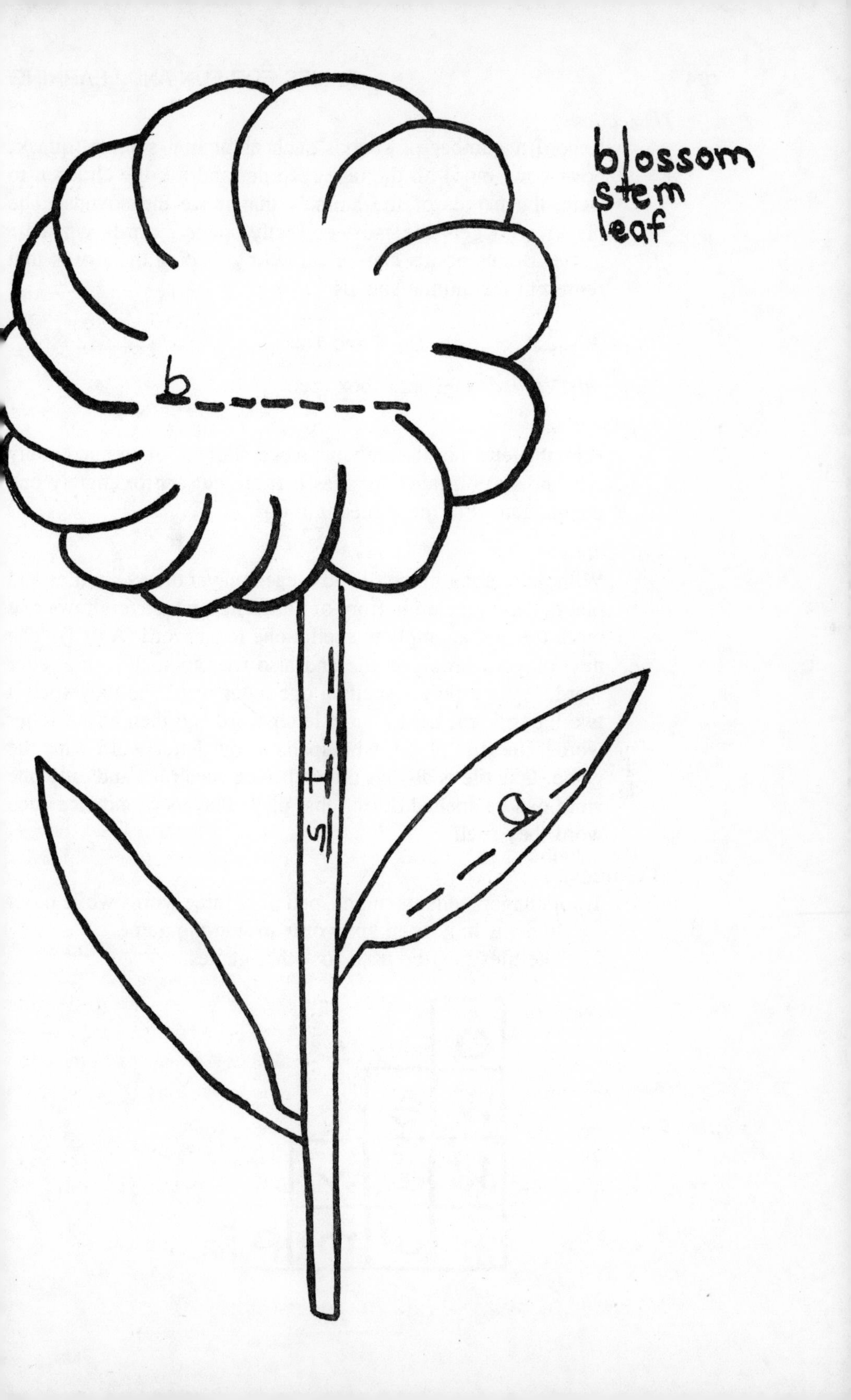
blossom
stem
leaf
b
s
a

Directions:

Record a number of sounds such as animal sounds (quack, bow-wow, moo) on the tape recorder and ask the children to write the names of the animals that made the sounds. The player who gets the most correctly spelled words wins the game. Bonus points can be earned by writing the words that represent the animal sounds.

Spell and Tell

Materials Needed: tagboard, box, pen

Preparation:

Print the letters of the alphabet (several of each letter and many A's and I's) on tagboard tiles that are cut approximately one inch square. Put these tiles in a box.

Directions:

Without looking in the tile box, each player draws six tiles and places them face up in front of him. The first player draws one more tile and attempts to spell a one letter word (A or I). The next player draws one tile and also tries to spell a one letter word. After a player spells a one letter word, he may spell a two letter word, next a three letter word and then a four letter word. The first player who spells a four letter word wins the game. One tile is always drawn before each play and only one word can be spelled during that play. Players pronounce each word they spell.

Variation:

1. Younger students might spell only three words while older students may spell six words to win the game.
2. The tiles may be used for other games.

RECYCLE INTO TIC-TAC-TOE

A disposable styrofoam tray can easily be recycled into the popular Tic-Tac-Toe board. When a teacher demonstrates how to recycle a number of throw-aways into games or crafts, students seem to become more aware of the recycling process and they seem to do more recycling on their own.

Materials Needed: disposable styrofoam tray, pipe cleaners of two different colors, crayons (optional)

Directions:

Turn a styrofoam tray upside down and draw a tic-tac-toe board on it. With a pipe cleaner, punch one hole in each section of the tic-tac-toe board to hold the pipe cleaner pegs in place. Cut pipe cleaners approximately three inches in length to use for the pegs, five pieces of each color. Roll up one end of the pipe cleaner a short way to form a small handle if you wish.

Variations:

1. Use trays for making peg boards, sewing cards, picture frames, and jewelry.
2. Put trays in the art center so that they are available to children for making crafts, games, etc.

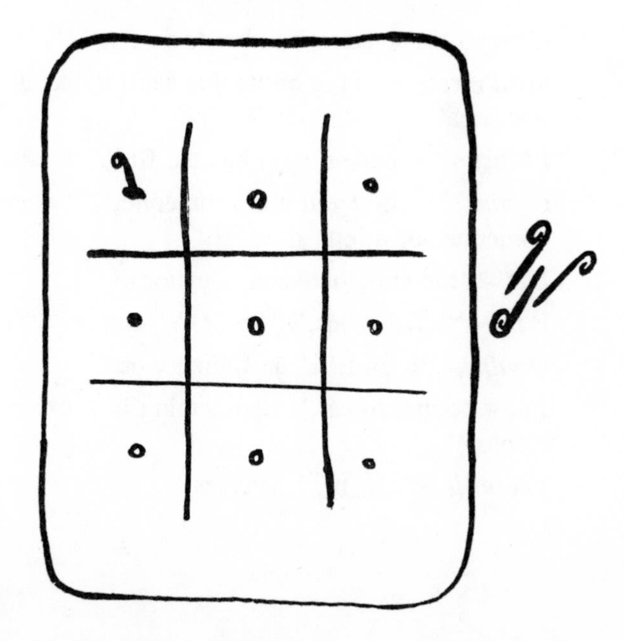

VOCABULARY GAME

You will probably have as much fun as your students when this game is played in your room. When students try to guess the meanings of unknown words, some of their definitions are very well thought out while others are just plain amusing! This game can help children build their vocabularies and increase awareness of the meaning of prefixes.

Materials Needed: blackboard, chalk, dictionaries, pencils and paper

Preparation:

Ask the children to look up a word in a dictionary which they think the other children do not know, and write down its definition on a piece of paper.

Directions:

The first child writes a word on the blackboard. The other children try to guess what the word means. If none of the children know the meaning of the word on the blackboard, the person who wrote it earns a point. If one of the players knows the meaning, he gets a point. The game continues until each player has had a turn. The player with the most points at the end of the time allowed wins the game.

Here are some children's definitions for the following words:

Artery - "a person who likes to do art," "a masterpiece"

Semi-circle - "a big circle that semi trucks drive in," "a rest area"

Flutist - "a person who has the flu"

Quaint - "when you meet someone," "when you know someone for a long time"

Lilt - "the stuff between your toes"

Vast - "left," "air," "quilt," "empty," "flat,"

Qualm - "a bird," "an Indian word"

Via - "paper towel," "something in Mexico," "vine," "color"

Versatile - "poem," "verses"

Chapter 6

Magic Mathematics

ACTIVITIES USING GEOMETRIC SHAPES

Children quickly learn to recognize the various geometric shapes as they trace, cut, and manipulate them in these informal experiences.

Materials Needed: white paper, construction paper of various colors, scissors, marking pens that are the same colors as the construction paper, cardboard

Preparation:

1. Cut large shapes of various colors from construction paper.
2. Cut identical, but slightly smaller, shapes from cardboard.
3. Place the cardboard shapes and marking pens in the math center so children can use them when they desire.

Directions:

Children trace around a cardboard shape with a marking pen on white paper, cut it out, and paste it on the corresponding color and shape of construction paper. For example, the *circle* made from the *blue* marking pen is pasted on the *blue* construction paper *circle* and the *square* made from the *red* marking pen is pasted on the *red* construction paper *square*.

If marking pens are used only for a special project such as this one, the project is more meaningful and fun. Marking pens are ideal for this project since they make a bright, wide line that is easy for children to see when they are cutting out the shapes.

Variations:

1. Students may be given smaller shapes so they can paste a number of them on a regular sheet of paper to create a design or picture.
2. Older children may trace the forms, cut them out, and write a description of the form on it.
3. Each child can choose a large geometric figure for a background to decorate with correlating geometric shapes. (If a diamond is chosen for the background, only diamond figures from any type of material are used.) The child then selects an appropriate title for the completed project.
4. Cut various geometric shapes into pieces to use as puzzles.

BANKING

This banking activity gives the teacher a chance to observe and help individual students as they work with money.

Materials Needed: a bank for each student such as one made from a plastic margarine or Country Kettle Cheese container, toy coins, paper and pencil for each child.

Preparation:

Cut a slot in the lid of the container so coins can be easily slipped through the slot.

Directions:

As the teacher tells a simple story about a child who saves his money, the children drop coins into their banks each time the teacher says a specified amount. At the end of the story, each child writes on paper an estimate of the amount he thinks is in his bank. Then he removes the lid, counts the value of the coins, and records the amount in his bank. When the teacher tells the answer he circles his correct answer(s).

Variation:

The teacher may wish to tell a story using only the participants' names in the story so each child has a different amount in his bank.

DIAL TIME AND TEMPERATURE

Telephones in the classroom help to arouse and to hold the attention of children as they study time and temperatures through the following activity.

Materials Needed: toy clock with movable hands, Bell Teletrainer or two toy telephones, room thermometer

Preparation:

1. The teacher introduces and reinforces one step at a time—one step at each session. For example, work on the "hour" until the child is familiar with the hour concept, then work on half hours, quarter hours, and finally five minute units. Too much information given at once is confusing and discouraging.
2. The clock and thermometer should be in view of all participants for a better learning situation.
3. The Bell Telephone Company, upon a teacher's request, will often deliver free of charge the Teletrainer—two activated telephones and a loudspeaker control unit.

Directions:

The child dials a designated number on his phone for finding out time or temperature information. (The child will enjoy making up the phone numbers himself.) The teacher answers the phone and conveys the correct information to the child (according to the toy clock and the room temperature). As a child learns to tell time and temperature, he may change roles with the adult, and answer the phone to give the correct information.

FRACTION PUZZLES

Playing with these puzzles help children become familiar with the names and symbols of fractions as the class compares parts with a whole.

Materials Needed: marking pens, tagboard, pizza or cake plates (or cardboard), large plastic lid (or cardboard), brass fastener

Preparation:

1. Divide four to eight plates into various equal parts (e.g. one in half, one in thirds, one in fourths, etc.) with a marking pen.
2. Make corresponding tagboard puzzle pieces that will cover all of the sections of the plates.
3. Divide a plate into unequal sections and label each part (e.g. ½, ⅓, ¼, etc.) Then make a spinner from a plastic lid and attach it to this plate with a brass fastener.

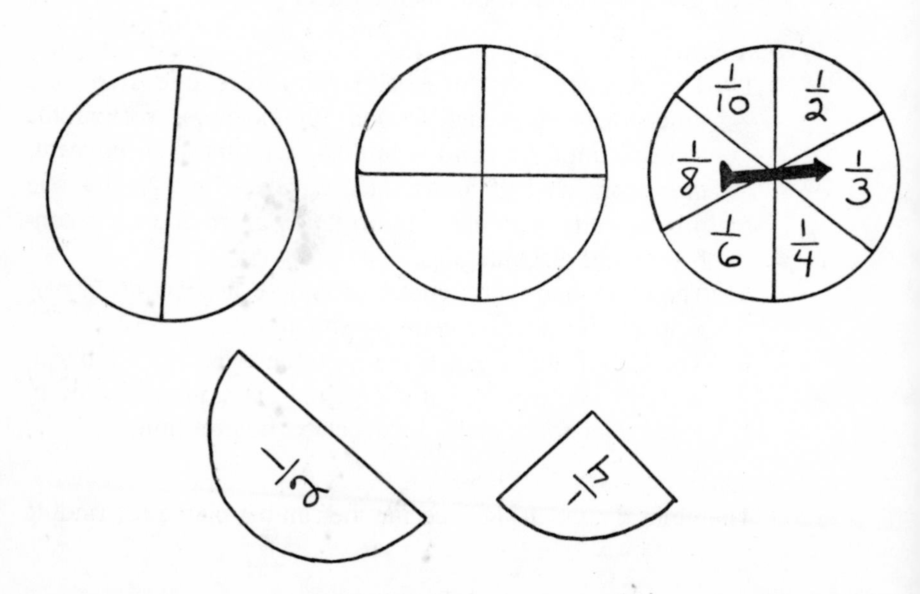

Directions:

Each player chooses an equal number of puzzle pieces and lays them in front of him. In turn, each player spins the spinner once. If the spinner lands on a fraction that corresponds with one of his puzzle pieces, he gets to lay that piece on the correct plate. The game continues in this manner until all of the parts make a whole. The first player to use all of his puzzle pieces is the first winner, with the game continuing until all participants have played their pieces of puzzle.

HOW MANY FLOWERS?

This simple aid allows a child to check his own answers since there are only enough holes in each vase to hold the correct number of flowers.

Materials Needed: paper or styrofoam cups, pipe cleaners, construction or crepe paper

Preparation:

1. Turn the paper cups upside down and decorate them to resemble vases.
2. Place a numeral between 1 and 10 (or between whatever numerals are desired) on the side of each vase.
3. Punch holes in the top of each vase (the bottom of each cup) to correspond with the numeral on its side.
4. Flowers are made by simply gluing or taping pipe cleaner stems to flowers cut from construction paper.

Directions:

The children use these flowers and vases as self-teaching aids by matching the number of flowers to the numeral on the vase. They then poke the correct number of flowers into the holes in the tops.

Variations:

1. Larger, more durable flowers can be put into larger cups and used simply as window or table decorations.
2. For one-to-one correspondence, children can place only one flower in each vase.
3. Enrich math vocabulary with "fewest," "less than," "more than," "most," etc.
4. Match the colored flowers to vases with the words "red," "yellow," etc., written on them.

INCH-BY-INCH

A child becomes more familiar with the measurement of "inches" when he moves inch-by-inch on a ruler with his pipe cleaner inch worm.

Materials Needed: a ruler and a die (or a cube with dots or numerals on it) for each set of partners, pipe cleaners

Preparation:

Cut a one inch piece of pipe cleaner for each player.

Directions:

Partners place a ruler in front of them on a table or a desk. The pipe cleaner worms are placed on "0." The first player tosses the die and moves as many inches as indicated by the dots on the die. If a child tosses a "six" he has to go back to "0" or if he is on his way down the ruler he has to go back to "12." The next player tosses the die and also moves. The first person who goes up to "12" and back to "0" wins one subgame. The person who wins two subgames out of three wins the total game.

Variations:

1. The game may be played on a yardstick.

2. A magnet can be used on a metal ruler to move from inch-to-inch.
3. A centipede can be used with centimeters.

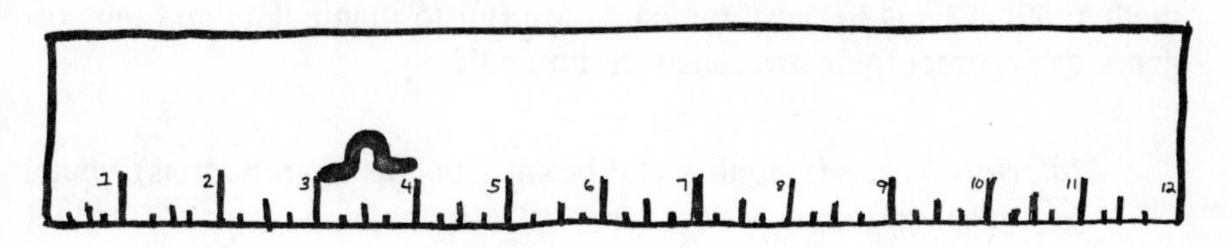

INDIVIDUAL MATH SLATE

These handy math slates, each made from a piece of cardboard covered with Contact paper, are useful to children for practicing math facts and for making geometrical shapes on their own.

Materials Needed: black or green Contact paper, cloth or tissue for eraser, soft chalk, cardboard, scissors

Directions:

Cover pieces of cardboard with Contact paper. The children may keep their math slates, chalk, and erasers in their desks to use for practicing math facts and other math problems.

Variations:

1. If a piece of black or green Contact paper is stuck on a table or at the top of a desk, it serves as a small slate for a student.
2. This slate can be used for reviewing reading and spelling words.
3. Glossy Contact paper can be used as a slate since some kinds of marking crayons and pens will work on it.

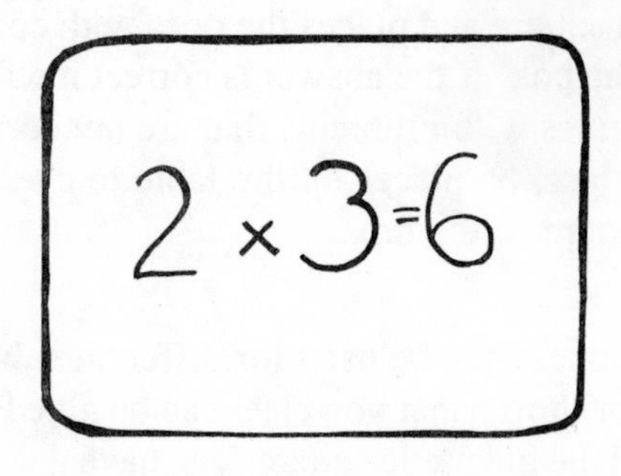

MAGIC MATH BOX

The students enjoy using these magic math boxes to practice their mathematical facts because the cards are fun to manipulate and the students can correct their own answers immediately.

Materials Needed: small metal boxes (such as from Sucrets), metal washers, magnetic strips, plastic bags, scissors, Contact paper, marking pencil, tagboard, glue

Preparation:

1. Use several colors and patterns of Contact paper to cover the metal boxes and make each unique.
2. Print one large numeral, from 1 through 10, on each box.
3. Cut pieces of the magnetic strip the same size and shape as the metal washers.
4. Cut pieces of tagboard that will cover each washer and magnetic piece. Glue each washer and magnetic piece inside of a piece of tagboard and then surround it with the tagboard so that it is completely invisible. Make the washers and the magnets as nearly the same size and weight as possible. (Two magnetic pieces may need to be placed together to equal the weight of one washer.)
5. On the outside of each tagboard square print a math problem. The correct answers for that box should be on the magnetic squares (for example, in box "3," the problem 6−3 would be a magnetic square while 3+2 would be a washer covered square).

Directions:

A child picks a magic math box, opens it, and removes the small squares from a small plastic bag. He reads the problem on each square and places the ones with correct answers on the top of the box. If the answer is correct it will adhere to the box. The squares with problems that are not correct for the numeral on that box, he places on the table to check later by seeing if they adhere to the box.

Variations:

These boxes may be used for different subjects. For example, a long or short paper vowel (ē) can be glued on top of the magic box and the magnetic squares can have a word containing these vowels on them.

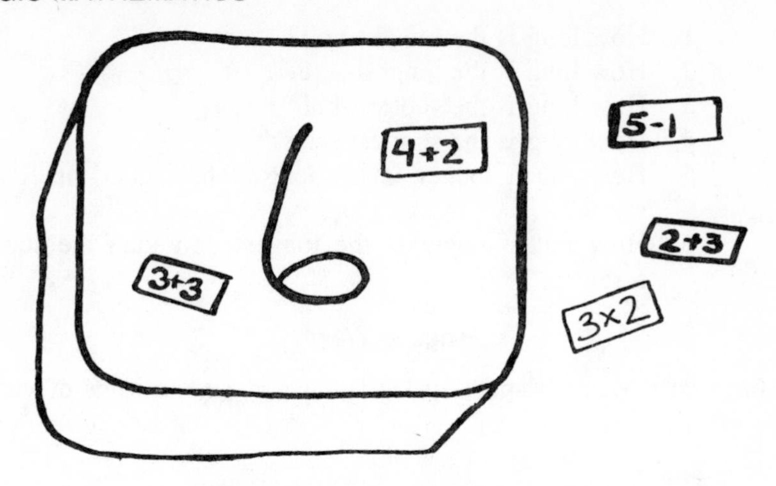

MANIPULATIVE MATH STORIES

Building math vocabulary and concepts through objects that children can manipulate is both meaningful and fun. Here are only a few of the many items and corresponding stories that a teacher can use for manipulative math stories. These stories can easily be modified for various levels of learning as well as for progressive learning experiences. Older children may write stories for younger children.

Screws and Bolts

Materials Needed: screws, bolts, box to hold screws and bolts

Directions:

The children count the screws and bolts in the box and answer the following questions:

1. How many screws are in the box?
2. How many bolts are in the box?
3. How many screws and bolts are there all together?
4. How many more screws are there than bolts?
5. How many fewer screws are there than bolts?

Measuring

Materials Needed: screws and bolts of different lengths, box to hold screws and bolts, rulers

Directions:

The children measure screws and bolts and answer the following questions:

1. How long is the longest bolt?
2. How long is the longest screw?
3. How long is the shortest bolt?
4. How long is the shortest screw?
5. How much longer is the longest bolt than the longest screw?
6. How much longer is the longest bolt than the shortest screw?

Rings to Weigh

Materials Needed: small spring balance scale, jar rings of various weights

Directions:

The children weigh various jar rings to find the answers to the following questions:

1. How many ounces do two jar rings weigh?
2. How many ounces do five jar rings weigh?
3. If you had ten jar rings, how many ounces would they weigh?
4. How much more do three jar rings weigh than two jar rings?
5. How much less does one jar ring weigh than four jar rings?

Catalog Shopping

Materials Needed: catalog, pencil and paper

Directions:

The children find birthday presents they would like to buy for a boy and for a girl.

1. How much does each birthday present cost?
2. How much do the presents cost together?
3. How much more does the present for the boy cost than the one for the girl?
4. How much less does the present for the girl cost than the one for the boy?

Flower Garden

Materials Needed: wallpaper, construction or other suitable paper, crepe paper, tape measure, yardstick, or ruler

Directions:

The children (or teacher) cut flowers from wallpaper or other suitable paper. Make crepe paper stems of different lengths and leaves. Tape the flowers on the wall or in the hall where the students can easily measure them to answer the following questions:

1. Which is the shortest flower?
2. Which is the longest flower?
3. How tall is the red flower?
4. How tall is the blue flower?
5. How many inches does the yellow flower need to "grow" to be as tall as the red flower?

Measure and Compare

Materials Needed: rice, measuring cups, pint and quart jars

Directions:

The children measure rice and answer the following questions:

1. How many cups of rice does it take to make a pint?
2. How many cups of rice does it take to make a quart?
3. How many half-cups of rice does it take to make one cup?
4. If a quart jar is filled with rice, how many cups will it fill?

Variation:

Change the stories for the metric system.

Telling Time

Materials Needed: small clock

Directions:

Put the long hand on 12 and the short hand on 3. What time is it? Continue with other hours and then with half hours.

Dozens and Dozens

Materials Needed: empty egg cartons, plastic or styrofoam eggs

Directions:

Put up to 12 eggs in an egg carton. The children answer the following questions:

1. How many eggs are in the carton?
2. How many eggs are there in a dozen?
3. How many more eggs do you need to make a dozen?
4. How many eggs are in a half dozen?
5. How many eggs do you need to add or subtract to make a half dozen?

Domino Facts

Materials Needed: dominoes, felt or paper

Directions:

Place a domino with six dots on the felt or paper. (Felt eliminates most noise.) Now place the domino with five dots on the felt. Answer similar questions:

1. Which domino has more dots?
2. How many more dots does the greater domino have?
3. Add the two dominoes together to find the total number of dots.

MEASURING AND COMPARING TIME UNITS

Children enjoy working with an automatic timer as they develop a better understanding of time units.

Materials Needed: an automatic timer

Directions:

The teacher and children discuss the words "second," "minute," and "hour." Ask the children to blink and explain that this takes about a second. Set the timer for one minute and tell the children to see what can be accomplished in one minute. (Some children may decide to see how far they can count before the timer rings.) Experiment with longer units of time: five minutes, ten minutes, etc. The children may then set the timer for various units of time.

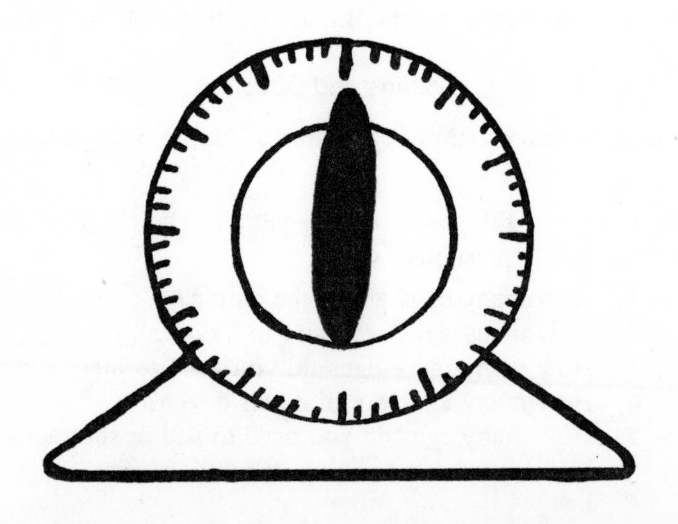

ONE-TO-ONE WITH SEALS

These seals make an excellent aid for children to participate in a one-to-one correspondence activity because each seal can hold only one ball on his nose at a time. This aid is also useful in perceiving left-to-right progression and mathematical stories.

Materials Needed: five-ten small juice cans, colored balls or balloons, scissors, white paper, pencil, paste

Preparation:

1. The teacher (or child) cuts white paper to fit around the outside of a three ounce juice can.
2. Paint or color the bottom half of the paper blue to resemble water (or use blue paper).
3. Trace the seal from the pattern on the next page, cut it out, paste it on the blue paper, and then paste the paper with the seal on it around the can.

One-to-One With Seal Pattern

Directions:

The children can use these seals and balls for discovering more about one-to-one correspondence as they place a ball on top of the seal's nose.

Variations:

1. Children may place the balls on the seals in the proper order for left-to-right progression.
2. Children can match each ball to the correct seal if the name of a color is printed on each can to correspond to the various colored balls. Or they can match the ball to a ribbon around the seal's neck.

SANDY FACTS

If you have a number of jar rings and several large sheets of sandpaper you can make this game in a matter of minutes. The students enjoy playing "Sandy Facts" and they learn some basic math facts without even realizing it.

Materials Needed: six large sheets of sandpaper (approximately eight x 12 inches), marking pen, four (or more) jar rings, pencil, score paper (or blackboard and chalk)

Preparation:

Write a numeral on the back of each sheet of sandpaper. These numerals can be one or more digits depending on the ability of the players. Sandpaper will adhere to the floor.

Directions:

A student places the sheets of sandpaper on the floor with the rough side down. Allow about four inches between each sheet. Each player has a turn in taking the four jar rings and attempting to throw them directly on the sheets of sandpaper from a designated position. When a jar ring lands directly on a sheet of sandpaper, the numeral on that sandpaper is the number of points earned. The points are added after each turn. The first player who reaches a designated number wins the game.

Variations:

For subtraction exercises, the players begin with a numeral such as "twenty" and subtract their subtotals. The first player

who gets "0" wins the game. Modify the game for multiplication and division, if desired.

STYROFOAM STACK

Recycle styrofoam cups into an aid that will encourage children to build towers from A-Z or from one to ten.

Materials Needed: styrofoam cups, crayon or marking pen, small pictures, scissors, and glue or crayons to decorate cups (optional)

Preparation:

1. Label the very bottom rims of styrofoam cups that are turned upside down. You may wish to use alphabet letters, ordinal numbers (like from 1-10), numbers to count by 5's, 2's, 10's, etc., and rhyming words.
2. If desired, cut out and glue a small appropriate picture on each cup above the symbol—a bear above the "B," five stars above "5," etc.

Directions:

Children stack a group of cups by placing one on top of another to progress through the alphabet or numbers, with the "a" or "1" at the bottom.

Two or more sets of cups containing rhyming words may be mixed together and then stacked with those that rhyme. For example, one set of cups can have "cat," "rat," "sat" on them and another set can have "hit," "bit," "pit," "sit." All eight cups are placed randomly on the table for the children to stack into two towers.

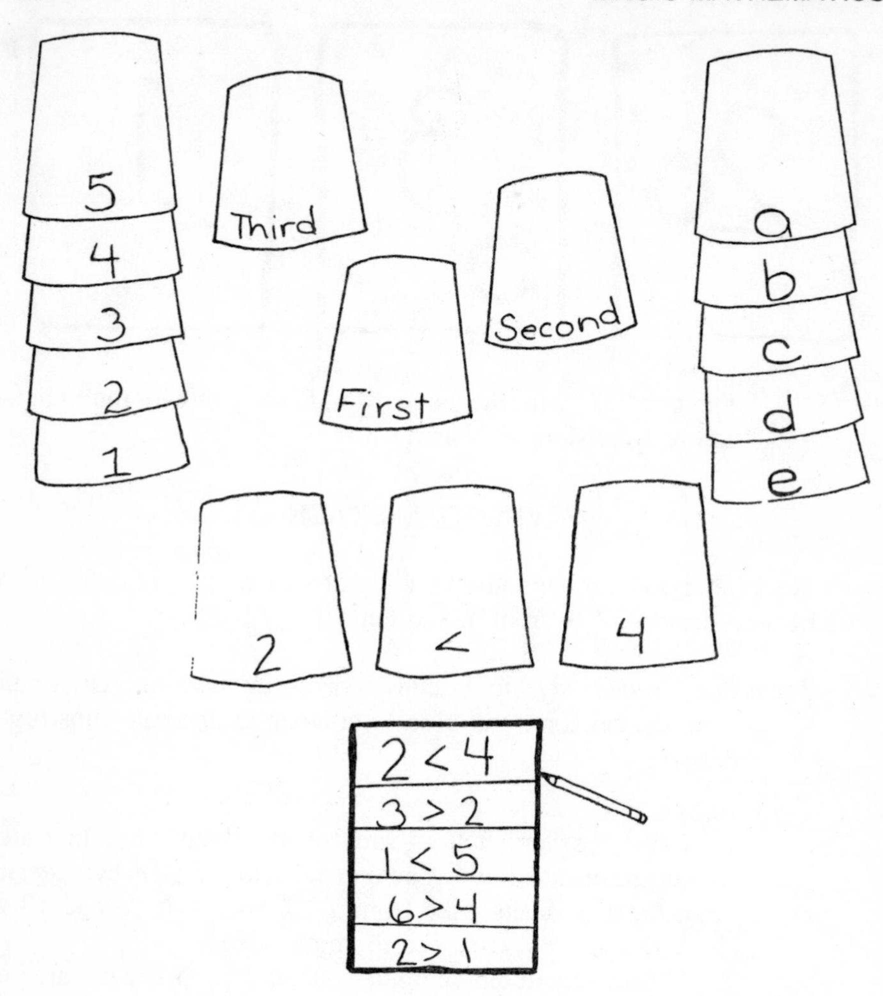
5
4
3
2
1
Third
First
Second
a
b
c
d
e
2
<
4
2 < 4
3 > 2
1 < 5
6 > 4
2 > 1

Chapter 7

Wonders in Science

COLOR FORMULA

Students like to learn about mixing colors by exploring on their own with this easy-to-make color formula.

Materials Needed: crepe paper strips (approximately two inches wide and preferably red, blue, and yellow), mixing containers, stirring utensil, paintbrush, ruler, paper, scissors, measuring spoons, three-by-five cards

Directions:

The children measure and cut a few inches of red, blue, and yellow crepe paper and place it in small containers. (Older students may be ready to mix more than the primary colors to arrive at shades and hues.) Approximately one-quarter teaspoon water for each two-four inches of crepe paper is stirred into each container until the paper's dye is dissolved. Students then remove the paper and mix two colors to create a third. If the formulas used to achieve new colors are recorded on three-by-five cards like the one below, children can mix their paint in the same proportions to obtain a secondary color that they can actually use.

4 inches yellow paper	
¼ teaspoon water	________
+	
2 inches red paper	
⅛ teaspoon water	________
=	
	total blend

COLORFUL SHADOWS

Children eagerly learn more about shadows as they experiment with the colored ones described below.

Materials Needed: colored transparent plastic (either purchased or a coffee can lid), marking pen, eye dropper (optional)

Directions:

Students cut shapes of their choice from colored, transparent plastic. As each shape is stuck on a sunlit window with a drop of water, beautiful colored shadows appear on the walls and

floor. Beginning experimenters can then proceed with these activities.

1. Watch and record the length of time the plastic shape sticks to the window.
2. Each child looks on the walls and floor to find the shadow from his plastic and traces it on paper.
3. Compare the plastic and its shadow in size and shape. (For easy comparison, the plastic can be traced on paper beside its traced shadow.)
4. To obtain a shadow with a design, part of the sunlight can be obstructed by drawing a design on the plastic shape with a marking pen.

GLURTCH

Students will have an opportunity to observe a chemical change and then work with the new product when they follow this fascinating formula.

Materials Needed: small mixing bowls (or cups), spoons, measuring spoons and cups, liquid starch, Elmer's glue, colander

Preparation:

1. If you are making Glurtch for the children, prepare the mixture prior to their experimentation session.
2. If the children are to make their own Glurtch, provide only the recipe and questions on a chart (or individual cards).
3. Experimenters may find that Glurtch possesses these and other properties:
   a. Two liquids (glue and starch) make a solid.
   b. Comic strip print transfers to Glurtch when the substance is pressed to a newspaper.
   c. Glurtch is lighter than clay.
   d. Patterns like those in fingerprints and certain fabrics (lace, embossed cotton) are retained by Glurtch.
   e. The tensile capacity of Glurtch is similar to gum.
   f. Glurtch is extremely malleable.
   g. When Glurtch is torn, it looks as if it had been cut by a knife.
   h. Glurtch bounces, but not as well as rubber.

i. Temperature changes occur in Glurtch as it is exposed to heat and cold.
j. Glurtch hardens when exposed to air for a length of time.
k. Objects made from Glurtch can be painted.

The class can discuss their findings and then store Glurtch in a plastic bag for later use.

Directions: (A sample card for students)

> *Glurtch*, A Mysterious Formula by Mary
>
> In a small container, mix one-half cup liquid starch with one-quarter teaspoon of salt. Pour one-quarter cup of Elmer's glue into this mixture. Beat about 30 strokes. Pour this mixture into a colander and let it set for 10 minutes to drain the excess starch. Knead until smooth.
>
> What have you observed about Glurtch?
>
> Why do you think this formula is called Glurtch?

GUESS MY SECRET

"Guess My Secret" is a game to help guide a small group of students into research and discussion of a particular science topic such as butterflies, the moon, dandelions, whales, etc. The topics are suggested by students.

Materials Needed: one piece of tagboard (approximately nine x 12 inches), appropriate book (or books), pencil or crayons and paper

Preparation:

1. Fold the tagboard two inches across one of the shorter sides to make a pocket at the bottom.
2. Obtain a suitable book and make it accessible to a small group of students who read on a similar level.
3. The game is a culminating activity to be played after the children in this group have had time to read the assigned book.

Directions:

After each child reads the assigned book, he writes a fact (secret) on one side of a sheet of paper; on the opposite side he draws a picture (or prints a large word) that conveys a clue about his secret fact.

The player who is "it" places his sheet of paper in the pocket with the clue picture (or word) facing the other players. The other players may ask questions of the player who is "it" if the questions can be answered by a "yes" or "no." The player who guesses the correct secretive fact gets a point. The person who is "it" can call on players at random or in turn from left-to-right. This rule needs to be set preceding the game. The player who earns the most points wins the game.

Variation:

This game can be played by using other subject areas such as literature or social studies.

INFORMATION BOARDS

Many gift wrapping papers are so interesting and attractive that they often motivate students to research whatever subjects are printed on the papers. They also make an appealing background for displaying the results of this research in learning centers and/or on bulletin boards.

Materials Needed: wrapping paper or wallpaper, glue, scissors, cardboard, paper and pencils

Preparation:

Glue a sheet of gift wrapping paper, such as one decorated with ladybugs or panda bears, to a piece of cardboard. Laminate this board, if desired.

Directions:

Children may use these boards for displaying factual information about the objects printed on the paper.

Variation:

Information Boards can be adapted to most subject areas at many learning levels.

MAGNETIC INTEREST BOX

This is an excellent manipulative aid to place in the science activity center because it captures the interest of students who are intrigued by magnets.

Materials Needed: small paperback book about magnets; small box; a piece of magnetic stripping (approximately 6 inches); some objects that magnets will attract: paper clips, small nails, bottle caps, small magnets, etc; some items that magnets will not attract: string, plastic, piece of wood, cork, etc.

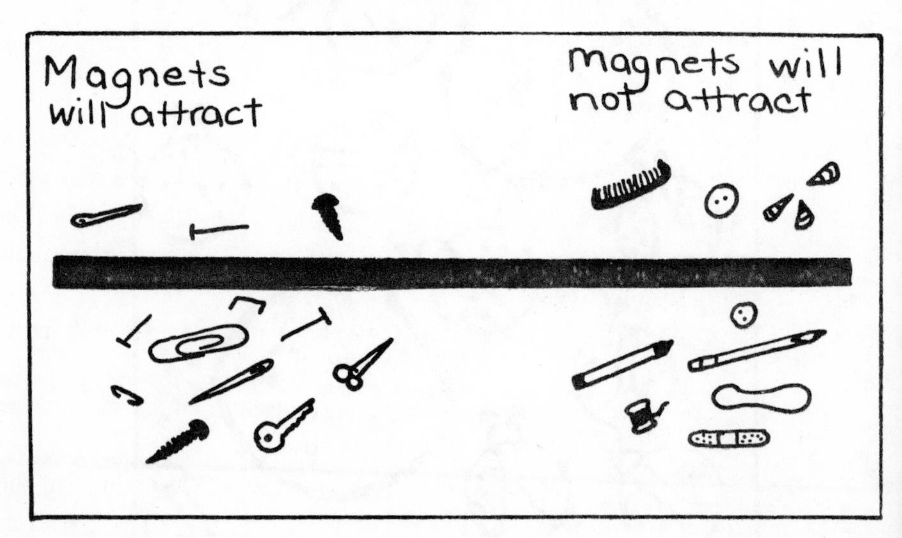

Directions:

Children read the book about magnets and experiment with the materials in the interest box.

Variations:

1. Interest boxes can be made for other units of study like rocks, seeds, insects, etc.
2. Experiment interest boxes contain cards of printed directions and all the materials required to perform those experiments.

MINI-UNIT GUIDE

The following mini-unit encourages children to use all of their senses as they see, hear, touch, taste, and smell popcorn. Such an activity allows a class to thoroughly examine a natural or raw object that later will be utilized in several forms in subject-related projects.

Materials Needed: corn popper, colored popcorn, oil, and salt (Other materials might be needed when children have organized their activities.)

Directions:

The children make plans for their popcorn unit by thinking of activities using popcorn in subject areas of their choice. Each group works independently on their projects before sharing the results with other groups.

Groups might come up with some of the following ideas; if not, the teacher may suggest them.

Literature: Locate and read stories and poems about popcorn.

Music: Compose and sing songs and listen to records about popcorn.

Physical Education: Play familiar games by substituting popcorn for usual objects, e.g. "Drop the Popcorn" (Drop the handkerchief). Invent new games using popcorn.

Science: Find information about popcorn—how it grows, what causes the kernels to pop, etc.

Math: Use different colors of kernels for making and comparing sets. Make an abacus.

Drama: Write and dramatize a play or story about popcorn and present it to other students.

Creative Writing: Write and record stories, poems (older students can use haiku), and myths (how popcorn happened to be).

Spelling: Learn to spell words that relate to popcorn. Partners exchange words to spell (kernel, caramel corn, hull, etc.)

Art: Culminating activity—create something from popcorn kernels and popped corn.

Mini-Unit Variations:

1. Beet Unit—Trace the lifecycle of a beet from the seed in the garden to the table in a different geographical location. Boil beets to make juice for painting.
2. Carrot Unit—Cook carrots and make carrot strips for comparing textures, taste, looks, fragrance, and the sound of them being dropped into a hot or cold pan. Play Hide-the-Carrot—One child hides the carrot and the other children find it. What vitamins are included in both raw and cooked carrots?
3. Potato Unit—Make potato candy (see recipe in Chapter 11). Play Hot Potato. Visit a potato factory. Grow a potato plant.

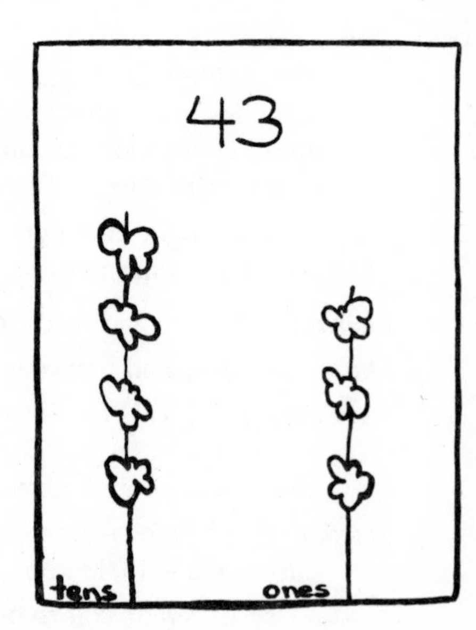

OBSERVATION CHART

Charts can be made to record information pertaining to the observations and discoveries that take place on a nature walk. As students keep these charts, they increase their awareness of specific objects in their environment.

Materials Needed: cardboard and pencil or crayon for each student

Directions:

Before going on a nature walk, the student divides his cardboard (approximately nine x 12 inches) into six or nine equal sections with his pencil. With their teacher's guidance, students discuss and perhaps list on the blackboard objects that are to be observed on the walk. Some of the properties of these objects might also be noted. This list might include specific leaves, insects, tree bark, birds' nests, spiders' webs, rotting logs, etc. After the discussion each child prints the name of an object in every square of his piece of cardboard, together with one or more questions on the object which he would like answered about the object.

During the walk each child looks for the listed objects and then attempts to discover the answer to his questions. The opposite side of the chart can be used for illustrations and/or additional information.

Variations:

A box can be substituted for the chart so that children can collect specimens of soil, rocks, bark, leaves, etc.

Spider's web Will there be an insect in the spider's web?	Maple leaf Will I see a Maple leaf?	Apple Tree
Bird's nest How many bird's nests will I see?	Butterfly	Pine Tree

REALIZATION

This assignment awakens children to the significance of the commonplace.

Materials Needed: one common object for each member of each group (or one object for each group): paper clip, rubber band, reinforcement ring, pencil, paper, eraser, and other suitable objects

Directions:

Divide students into equal groups of four to six and give each group a different object. Within a designated time limit of a few minutes to one-half hour, the groups examine their objects and write brief reports. (If research is done, allow the longer time period.)

The culminating activity may be sharing the information which may consist of what, when, where, why, and how the particular item was manufactured for market.

Variations:

1. To illustrate the comparison of an item among groups, the teacher can give the students identical objects to evaluate and discuss.
2. Individuals or partners may wish to pursue this activity at their discretion as a special interest project.

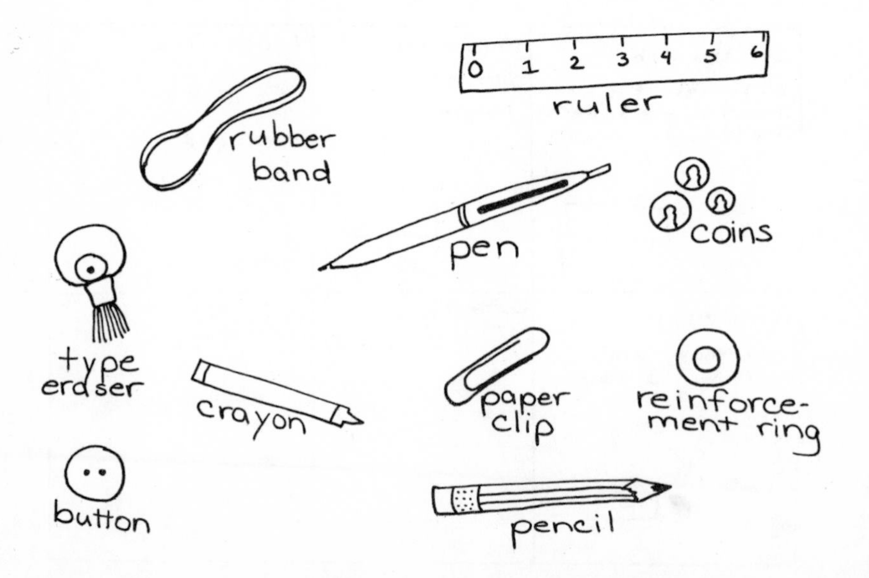

RECYCLE TO CONSERVE

Because students are concerned about ecological problems, they will enjoy this activity which actually allows them to recycle potential discards.

Materials Needed: different kinds of throw-away items, a large box to hold throw-aways, glue, scissors, crayons

Preparation:

1. Print "RECYCLING BOX" on a large, gaily decorated box.
2. Select, decorate, and label a shelf "RECYCLE TO CONSERVE" to display the recycled art and craft projects.
3. Ask students to bring throw-aways to contribute to the box.

Directions:

As the teacher or a child holds up each throw-away in several different positions, the children try to think of how they can recycle it. For example, when a styrofoam tray is shown, it can be visualized as a pegboard, a puzzle, a sewing card, a geometrical figure form, a paint tray, or a cutting board for vegetables.

After the brainstorming session, the box is passed from one child to another so that each can choose a throw-away for his project.

Variation:

The game of "Guess What I'm Thinking" can be used with the Recycling Box. One child can choose an object from the box, imagine it recycled as something else, write the word on a

slip of paper, and call on students who guess what recycled object he has in mind. For example, a child holds up a plastic fabric softener bottle with a handle, writes "pitcher" on the paper, and calls on classmates to guess. The child who says "pitcher" becomes "it" and chooses another object from the box. If no one guesses the correct object, "it" takes a different item from the box and play resumes until someone guesses correctly.

SCIENCE EXHIBIT GUIDE

A science exhibit prepared for another class and/or parents facilitates the inclusion of many topics at all age and ability levels. Teachers and students can organize and present such an exhibit with minimal effort when using the following guide.

Materials Needed: science books with good illustrations and experiments, carrels or listening center dividers on tables (or other suitable dividers), science materials for constructing exhibits, bulletin board space, crayons or marking pens, scissors, paper or other material suitable for backgrounds, and materials for posters.

Directions:

Science students can either work alone or in partners to plan, organize, and participate in a science exhibit. Preliminary work includes installing suitable backgrounds for projects on the sides and backs of the carrels, on bulletin boards, and on any other display areas. Mobiles, posters, and invitations can be made to advertise the affair.

The tables, with exhibits inside dividers, are placed so that people can easily walk around and view all the displays. (Those who conduct experiments may require more table space than carrels allow.)

During the exhibit, participants who do not conduct experiments may want to stand near their projects to discuss them with passers-by who wish to comment or ask questions. Some students may place a tape recorder that explains their exhibit near their science display.

Variation:

Other exhibits can include simple, original inventions for an invention fair, recycled projects for an ecology exhibit, and students' hobbies for a hobby exhibition.

Chapter 8

A Journey in Social Studies

A GUIDED TOUR

This "You Are There" approach to learning is very flexible as it adapts to use in imaginary places of interest: school, museum, store, art gallery, governmental office, airport, historical area, factory, television or movie studio.

Materials Needed: a number of books of the Cinderella theme from a variety of countries

Directions:

Upon completion of preparation of a project to be shared with parents, community, or another class, a guided tour can be conducted by one of several students. Such an informal setting encourages many volunteers to participate as readers or demonstrators.

The following example works especially well when studying literature from other countries. Either several stories about the same theme or several separate stories or poems may be used.

"Variations of the Folk Tale" (Cinderella)

Usher in a theater: "Hello, friends, from ____________. We're delighted you came to hear our folk tale readings today.

I'm ___________, your usher, and I'll be taking you to four rooms (can be four areas within a classroom) where you will hear someone reading a portion (or all if desired) of a story with a "Cinderella" theme. Each time we move to a different room, the story will continue as it was written in another country. Even though the stories are almost alike, characters and even titles change. (There are hundreds of tales, which students can locate in the library, based on the "Cinderella" theme.) Now let's go into this room so we can hear the beginning of the "Cinderella" story from France (for example).

(First reader tells the first portion of the tale as it is told in France.) Usher (standing):

"In the next room we'll continue with the story as it is told in __________."

(Second reader stands and reads his rehearsed portion.) The usher and readers continue in this manner with four (or more) countries and versions.

Variations:

1. In an imaginary museum, interested students can provide and explain different kinds of rocks, fossils, old tools, etc.
2. In an imaginary historical area, some students can explain the history of that area to other students by using posters, maps, filmstrips, etc.
3. In an imaginary art gallery, one or more students can explain each painting and tell about the artist.

CHILDREN OF OTHER LANDS

These special interest projects dealing with people of other lands can be pursued by volunteers who pass their new knowledge onto others.

A Magnetic Time Line

Materials Needed: magnetic stripping for a time line, paper clips, construction paper, time line cards cut approximately five x five inches, and books and other informational materials that relate to the country the student is studying.

Preparation:

1. Make books and materials available to the students for research purposes. (Older students can use the card catalog to find some of their own.)
2. Fasten approximately a yard of magnetic stripping horizontally on a blackboard, bookcase, or other suitable place so that students can later demonstrate their imaginary time line projects.

Directions:

A student takes an imaginary trip to a country such as Ireland. First, he reads books, views filmstrips, interviews people who have visited there, etc. to find out as much information about this country and its people as possible. Next, he plans and prepares time line cards that describe his trip (of a day, a week, or more) with brief statements and/or illustrations. Paper clips hooked through the tops of these cards will stick to the magnetic strip to form a time line. Finally, the student uses his cards to explain his adventures to a group of students or to an entire class.

Variation:

1. This idea can be modified to take place in a different state rather than a country.
2. The time line can be used for a number line, a life cycle line, or a historical event line.

Visitors From Another Country

An activity for two (or more) different classes.

Materials Needed: (Older Students): books, filmstrips, etc., for research; simple costumes (see ideas for costumes in Chapter 3); map of the country to be studied

(Younger Students): a few books about the country and its people (the same country as the older students study), paper or other suitable material for an invitation. Other materials may be needed as planning progresses.

Directions:

A number of older students do as much research as possible on a country such as Scotland. For example, the children might decide to make simple plaid costumes, design a cardboard bagpipe, locate a bagpipe record to play, and illustrate Scotland's flag.

The younger students might write an invitation and make plans for their Scottish friends' visit. This may involve decorating a long sheet of white paper to place on the floor for everyone to sit around, creating a simple centerpiece, and preparing food. The younger students act as hosts and hostesses for their Scottish friends—the older students. They may also think of questions which they will want to ask their guests.

When the older students arrive, a younger student may ask them to join the class around the table where everyone discusses Scotland and its people.

Variation: Two classes may each study a different country and then share their information at a visitation.

ECONOMICS AT WORK

Students reinforce and expand their understanding of the concepts of work, time, and money in this activity. They work on an assembly line in an automobile factory, park in a parking lot for a specific length of time, and go on a shopping spree to buy their choice of books and games.

Materials Needed: toy money, clock, books, games, marking pen, masking tape, cardboard boxes for a number of automobiles, and a cash register (optional)

Preparation:

1. To make certain that the cars have an opportunity to dry, the teacher helps arrange and set in motion an assembly line at least a day before the shopping spree.
2. The teacher helps students divide into groups for setting up a parking lot and two stores. (Merchandise can be priced by using marking pens on masking tape that is taped to the games and books.)

At the Factory

Students work on an assembly line, in shifts, at the factory. For example, one worker might fold the top and bottom flaps inside the box. Others may be responsible for painting a portion of each box, while the last person may place the car on a newspaper to dry. Workers receive toy money in accordance with parking and shopping costs.

At the Parking Lot

While some students work as clerks in the stores and as parking lot attendants, others drive their cars to the parking lot where they get tickets with numerals on them before going shopping. The parking lot attendant records the numeral and the time that each car arrives. (He might charge one cent a minute.)

At the Store

Students spend the money they have earned on books and games of their choice, saving enough money to pay for their parking. They return to the parking lot to pick up their cars and pay the parking fee.

At Home

After students return home to play their games and read their books, other students may use the cars for their shopping spree.

EMOTIONAL RESPONSES

Children become more aware of their own emotions, values, and attitudes and those of their classmates through the informal conversations that take place during this activity.

Materials Needed: paper (approximately 12 x 18 inches), crayons

Directions:

Fold a piece of paper in half. On the outside of the paper draw a happy face with the word "happy" near it. Inside the folded paper, draw a picture that shows why this person is happy. If desired, a sentence or paragraph may be written about this happy person.

Guessing Game: One student shows only his "happy face" while the others ask questions (that can be answered by either "yes" or "no") until they guess the information that is on the inside (e.g. Is this person happy about something good to eat?).

Variations:

1. Students may choose words such as sad, excited, surprised, pleased, rude, angry, embarrassed, and mean instead of happy.
2. The directions for this idea can be placed on a card in a learning center so students can do this activity during their free time.

FROM POSTCARD TO MAP

This map study activity is an excellent way to utilize postcards with a small or large group of students at almost every level of learning.

Materials Needed: postcards from many places (or the area under study), books about the geographical locations pictured (optional), a box to hold the postcards, and large maps of the regions.

Directions:

Classmates draw postcards from the box at random and study both the pictures and facts. They exchange data by giving oral reports and matching the places of interest to their locations on maps. If time allows, the students can find additional information in related books.

Variations:

1. Younger students may look at the postcards, discuss them, and help the teacher locate the place of interest on the map.
2. Older students may research and make an oral or written report about the places of interest on the postcards.
3. A student might have the opportunity to earn a postcard if he writes or gives a report about the place that is portrayed on the card.

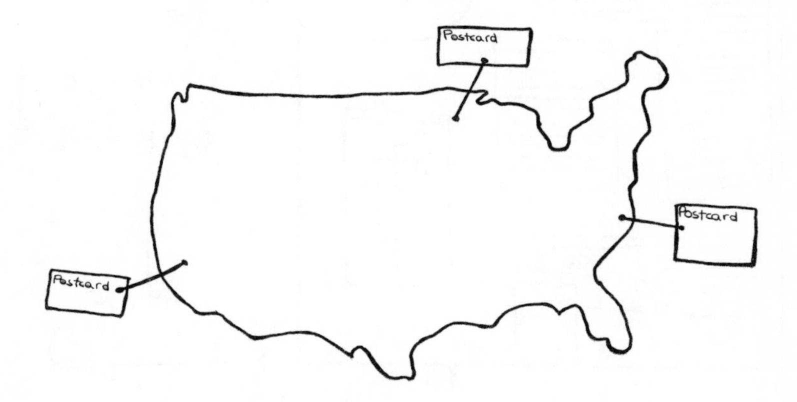

INFORMATION BUILDINGS

This simple but effective idea may provide just the motivation some students need to become involved in the study of a political entity.

Materials Needed: moist towelettes or paper, crayons or colored chalk, a box for a building (such as a tall Kleenex box), glue, toothpick or Popsicle stick for flagpole, newspapers and news magazines, clay to hold flag (optional), free pamphlets from states upon request (optional)

Directions:

A student or partners select from a current unit of study an area (city, state, or nation) and one of its landmarks (State Capitol for a state, Eiffel Tower for France, Carpenter's Hall for Philadelphia). He then designs a building to resemble the real one and covers it with short, relevant newspaper and magazine clippings.

The area's flag can be fashioned by coloring on a moist towelette, which is glued to a stick and placed in clay near or on the building.

Class members may display their information buildings for each other or for special events (P.T.A., National Education Week, etc.)

LIST OF CAREERS

The following list of careers may be helpful for the "Pocket-A-Career" and "Puzzle Work" activities in this chapter. It can also be used for developing an on-going file of information on careers.

Accountant
Actor
Airport Control Tower Operator
Archaeologist
Architect
Astronaut
Baker
Ballerina
Bank Clerk
Baseball Player
Beautician
Biologist
Blueprint Reader
Boxer
Bus Driver
Cab Driver
Candy Maker
Captain of a Ship
Carpenter
Cartoonist
Chemist
Circus Performer
Clown
Computer Operator
Dairy Farmer
Deep-sea Diver
Delivery Person
Dental Assistant
Detective
Dietitian
Dishwasher
Doctor
Druggist
Drummer
Editor
Electrician
Engraver
Environmental Health Assistant
Explorer
Farmer
File Clerk
Fingerprint Expert
Fireman
Food Inspector
Football Player
Forest Ranger
Garbage Collector
Geologist
Glass Blower
Government Leader
Greenhouse Manager
Guitarist
Health Inspector
Homemaker
Hotel Manager
House Painter
Interior Decorator
Interpretor
Insurance Agent
Janitor
Jeweler
Journalist
Judge
King
Key Punch Operator
Laboratory Technician
Landscape Gardner
Lawyer
Leather Worker
Librarian
Lumberman
Mailman
Masoner
Meatcutter
Miner
Museum Guide
Newscaster
Newspaper Reporter
Nurse
Occupational Therapist
Oceanographer
Optometrist
Patrolman
Pharmacist
Photographer
Pilot
Plumber
Professor
Queen
Radio Announcer
Rancher
Salesman
Sculptor
Sign Painter
Teacher
Trucker
Typist
Watchmaker
Weatherman
Welder
Writer
Umpire
Usher
X-ray Technician
Ventriloquist
Veterinarian
Violinist
Yardmaster
Zookeeper

POCKET-A-CAREER

Students become acquainted with the tools of a cross-section of careers as they enthusiastically gather materials to fill shoebag pockets.

Materials Needed: transparent shoeholder, masking tape, catalogs, magazines, construction paper, scissors, (see list of careers in this chapter)

Directions:

Each pocket of a transparent shoebag is decorated and labeled with masking tape to represent a career. For example, the pocket with a fireman's picture on the outside can contain a piece of real hose, a paper boot inscribed with information about his job, an envelope of related pictures, and toy tools (ax, ladder, truck, etc.).

After the children help collect enough career materials to fill the pockets, they can place them together in a box for classroom use. Students with free time can then attempt to sort the items and return them to their places.

Variations:

1. The objects and pictures can be labeled, using a marking pen or masking tape, to reinforce reading vocabulary.
2. Pockets can be redecorated for different careers as often as desired.

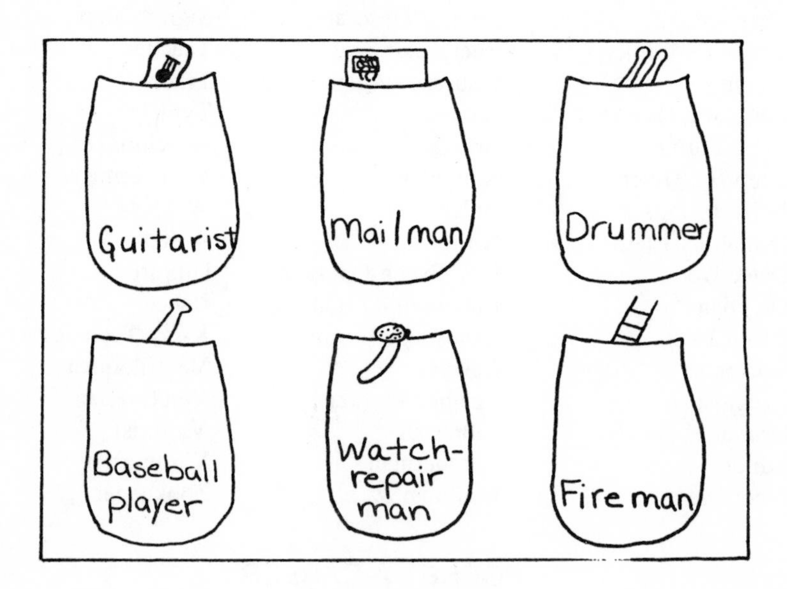

PUZZLE WORK

This interesting puzzle permits a student to choose and study careers at his own level of ability and at his own rate of speed.

Materials Needed: a large sheet of tagboard, marking pen, tracing paper, pencil, crayons, scissors and references like magazines, old workbooks, newspapers, books, etc.

Preparation:

1. Illustrate a puzzle on the tagboard by drawing dark, wide lines with a black marking pen.
2. Locate books and other materials for research purposes. (See list of careers in this chapter.)
3. Print the name of a different career inside each section of the puzzle. Make certain that the careers that are named correspond to the available research materials.

Directions:

A student chooses and traces one of the pieces of the tagboard puzzle on his tracing paper. On the *back* of this traced piece of puzzle, he prints the name of that career. Then he searches for pictures and/or information about this career and glues them on the *front*. When this activity is completed, he cuts out his piece of puzzle and glues it on to the matching tagboard piece. When the entire tagboard puzzle is filled, the participating children may wish to share the career information with other members of the class.

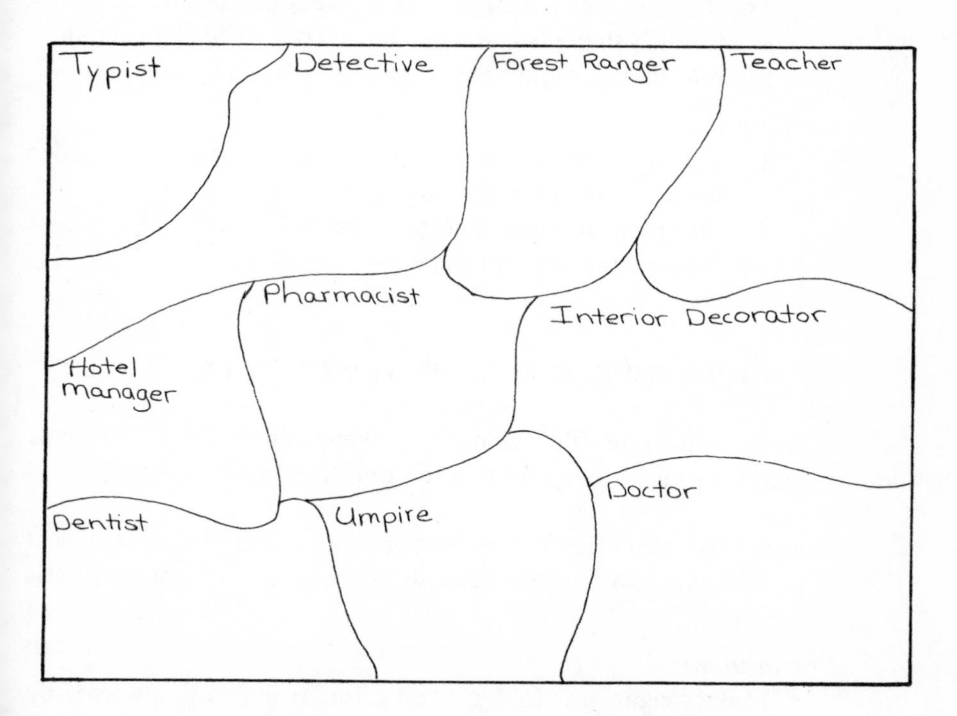

RADIO AS A MEDIUM

Marcia Miller and I enjoyed working with the students on this unit. Actually, we didn't do much more than set the environment for the activity and tape the program since the students organized and prepared the radio program.

Materials Needed: empty box, tape recorder, library books and films about radios.

Preparation:

1. The teacher and children discuss the radio and radio programs.
2. If possible, take the class to tour a radio station.

Directions:

After discussion and a tour of a radio station (optional), students work individually or in groups to plan a radio program. They decide which part of a radio program to present: news, music, weather, interviews, recipes, etc. After writing their own stories and advertisements, each group rehearses its segment separately and then with the class.

The teacher tapes the program and places the recorder in a play radio which students can make from a box. The class can then listen to their program and then play it for another class.

Variations:

1. The children can take turns taking the tape and recorder home for their families to enjoy.
2. The radio program can be presented at a P.T.A. "Open House" meeting for parents.

SOMETHING OLD-SOMETHING NEW FILE

Making Something Old—Something New folders for a file helps arouse children's curiosity about specific objects and their history.

Materials Needed: file folders (or paper cut and folded to represent folders), marking pen, box to hold folders, magazines, scissors

Preparation:

Make magazines, folders, and a file available to students by placing them in the learning center. As the children find appropriate old and new materials in school and at home, they can complete these folders and establish additional folders.

Directions:

Glue on one-half of a folder (inside) an object or a picture of something old and on the other half something new that correlates with the object on the opposite half. For example, one-half of the folder contains some old postcards and the opposite half contains some new postcards. Older students may research an object, writing down some interesting facts or a brief report on paper and gluing the paper to the front or back of the folder. The name of each item can be written at the top of the folder with a marking pen.

Variation:

A bulletin board display may be designed with these old and new folders when enough are completed.

TOUR AND TRAVEL AGENCY

Purposeful research can be encouraged through this tour and travel agency project. Students explore areas and design posters to promote places of interest in the community, state, nation, or in the world after students have discussed a travel agency. If possible, a class field trip to a tour and travel agency would contribute to the success of this activity.

Materials Needed: tour and travel booth (three tables might be arranged to represent booth), materials for designing creative posters

Directions:

A dramatization between a travel agent and an interested party of prospective vacationers or tourists takes place in a modified tour and travel agency. A travel atmosphere is easily depicted through creative posters about places of interest. A vacationer first chooses the poster that appeals to him and the student that

designed it becomes the travel agent, promoting his particular interest or topic to the other students. (The agent will have done considerable research on his topic in addition to having designed the poster.) When a student has had a turn to tell what he knows about his topic, a different vacationer chooses another poster and the person who designed it becomes the agent, continuing this procedure until all of the students have had a turn. This activity makes an excellent culminating program for other classes or parents. Each student may enjoy designing a suit or dress box to represent a suitcase. The suitcase is used for holding various items that are correlated with his topic and that can be displayed when he is the Agent. Two or three students may work together on one topic.

VOTE FOR A BOOK

Books become very special when they are up for a vote. Since this activity is to encourage reading books relating to a certain subject, it is important that the teacher provide books at the reading level of each participating child.

Materials Needed: factual books on students' reading levels (fewer books than students), book ballots (see Book Ballot in illustration), scissors

Preparation:

1. Trace and duplicate the sample Book Ballot (or design) your own Book Ballot.
2. Place Book Ballots in a box or on a bulletin board that is easily accessible to students.

Directions:

Students read books of their choice during their spare time. (Some stories may be taped.) At the end of a given length of time each interested student votes for his favorite book on the book ballot. The students, with teacher guidance, discuss and decide upon special activities that will take place when the voting is over to honor the winning book. For example, students might decide to have the winning book read or recorded by the teacher or a parent, displayed in a special place, or used for dramatization.

Name of a book

Chapter 9

Creative Art Expression

ART CENTER SUPPLIES

A box with dividers, each section labeled to hold a certain kind of material, works well for organizing and storing some of the supplies in the art center. The following list of supplies can be used in the art center.

- aluminum foil
- aquarium rocks
- baking cups
- bark
- beads
- beans (dried)
- bottle caps
- boxes
- burlap
- buttons
- cardboard
- carpet remnants
- cedar chips
- cellophane
- cereal
- chalk
- clay
- clothespins
- coffee grounds (dried)
- Contact paper
- cork
- cotton
- craft trims
- crayons
- crepe paper
- disposable trays
- dowel sticks
- egg cartons
- eggshells
- fabric scraps
- fake fur scraps
- feathers
- felt
- foam scraps
- gift wrapping
- glue
- grains
- grass (fake)
- hangers
- hardware cloth
- interfacing fabric
- jar rings
- jewelry
- juice cans
- keys
- Kleenex
- leather scraps
- leaves

lipstick lids
macaroni
magazines
marbles
match boxes
milk filters
moist towelettes
nails
net
newspapers
nut cups
nut shells
nylon stockings
orange peelings (dried)
paint
paper cups
paper cut in different shapes
paper plates
paper punch
pine cones
pipe cleaners
pizza plates
plaster of Paris
plastic bottles
potato chip canisters
records (old)
reinforcement rings
ribbons
rice
sacks
sandpaper
screen
seashells
seeds
sego
shellac
sponges
spools
stickers
stones
straws
string
tapioca
thread
tissue paper
toothpicks
trinkets
twigs
valentines
vinyl cloth scraps
wallpaper
watermelon seeds
wax paper
wax paper tubes
wire
wood scraps
yarn
zippers

ART EXPRESSION WITH SCRAPS

Here are a number of ways to use scraps to stimulate creative expression in art.

Materials Needed: paper, crayons, any type of scraps that can be glued on paper such as yarn, bias tape, fabric, jar rings, plastic bag closures, etc.

Preparations:

1. Ask students to bring scraps from home.
2. Put scraps in a box and place them in the art center.

Directions:

Activity 1: Students may choose two pieces of scraps from the scrap box to glue on a piece of paper for a portion of their picture or design. The students may complete their project with crayons, paint, chalk, or a combination of all three of the media.

Activity 2: The box of scraps can be passed around so that a student can draw an item from the box without looking. This item may be included in a student's illustration.

Activity 3: Place a variety of scraps in a shallow box or on a tray so that students can choose several of them to glue on a piece of paper for a design. They may finish their project with crayons or paint.

yarn

plastic closure

ART LINE

A wire art line spanning the classroom inspires students to both read and create as they eagerly scan its captions for material to illustrate.

Materials Needed: wire, construction paper, marking pen, crayons (chalk and paint may also be used), small clothes pins

Preparation:

Provide a wire line for hanging papers that have captions printed on them.

Directions:

Volunteers suggest captions for the teacher (or a classmate) to print on sheets of construction paper. These and some blank sheets are suspended from the wire.

At a student's discretion, he removes the paper of his choice from the line and either creates his own theme and picture or illustrates a caption. Completed pictures can be returned to the line for viewing. When a paper is taken home, it is replaced by either a blank sheet or one with a new caption.

Once this idea is introduced, older students may keep the line filled by writing the captions on the papers when needed.

Some captions might read as follows:

A Funny Trick
Candy
What I Like To Do
Grandma
I Laughed and Laughed
I Wish. . .
My Favorite Food
My Imagination Fun
Glub, Glub, Glub!
Me, Myself, and I
My Friends
Yes, Little Puppy!
Very Good!
My Best Toy
I Forgot To. . .
My Favorite Television Show
Grandpa
My Favorite Story
An Interesting Triangle
A Birthday Party
A Very Unusual Animal
See!
My Family
My Favorite Neighbors
Something I've Never Seen
Clowning Around

Variation:

1. The line may be used for a variety of paper clothing, labeled for building vocabulary. The children may be designers and fashion clothing with crayons or paint for an art activity.
2. Titles can be written on writing paper and hung on the line so that they are available to the students for their original stories.

COFFEE MONOCHROMATICS

Coffee grounds and instant coffee provide an opportunity for the teacher to informally introduce the word and concept of ''monochromatic'' in art.

Coffee Grounds

Materials Needed: used, dried coffee grounds, white glue, paper, pencil (optional)

Directions:

The children plan a design or picture for their paper, with pencil if desired. They decide which areas to cover with the coffee grounds and then spread the glue only on those spots. Next they sprinkle the dried coffee grounds over these areas, letting them dry, and shaking off any excess grounds.

Variation:

These pictures become colorful when tempera paint is used to cover some or all of those sections without grounds.

Instant Coffee Paint

Materials Needed: instant coffee, water, paper, paintbrush

Directions:

Mix a small amount of instant coffee with a small amount of water. Paint a coffee design with a brush or with any other suitable object. Use thick coffee paint first, and then thin with more water for a lighter coffee color.

CREPE PAPER ROPE

There will be plenty of volunteers to assist the teacher in beating crepe paper into rope for functional art projects.

Materials Needed: crepe paper strips about two or three inches wide and approximately four or five yards long, electric mixer which has separate beaters (only *one* beater is used), paper, crayons or paint

Directions:

Tie one end of the crepe paper strip to the bottom of *one* beater. The teacher operates the mixer while a student holds

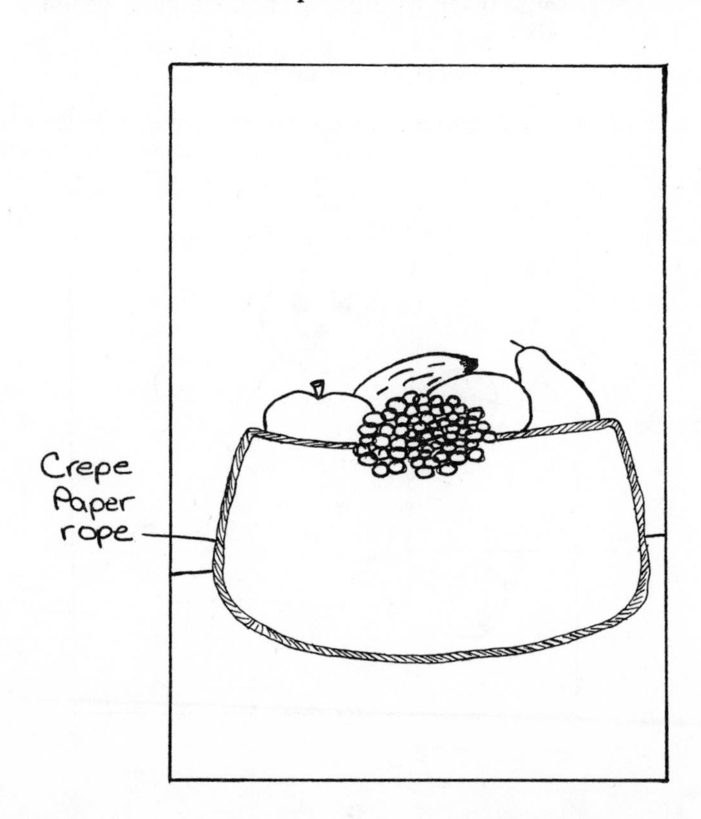

the free end of the strip, stretching it quite tightly. Turn the mixer on low to twist the strip into a rope. Tie a knot at each end. Here are a few ways to use the rope:

1. Put glue on the outside of boxes or cans and wind the rope around them to make colorfully trimmed containers to hold jewelry, pencils, pins, thread, rubber bands, buttons, hair pins, curlers, stamps, etc.
2. Glue rope on paper to form an outline. The inside of the design can be colored or painted.
3. Make any size numerals and alphabet letters.
4. Use the crepe paper outside as a jump rope or a "finish" line in a race.

LOVE THOSE LIDS!

Since discarded plastic lids and caps are so plentiful, students have an ample supply of plastic in many shapes and sizes.

Materials Needed: plastic lids or caps, food coloring or tempera, white glue

Preparation:

A special formula is needed to paint the lids because pure tempera will loosen from plastic when it dries. The following formula card can be made accessible to the students:

Plastic Glue Formula

Mix together:
- ¼ cup glue
- 2 or 3 drops of food coloring or dry tempera (food coloring gives a glossy finish)
- 1 teaspoon of liquid soap or water

Directions:

Here are some of the ways to creatively utilize discarded lids and caps:

1. Large lids, like those from margarine and coffee cans, may be used as backgrounds for painting pictures with the plastic glue formula.

2. Cover a lid with white glue and let it dry until it's clear; paint on this coating with tempera.
3. Cut shapes out of the lids and either paint them with the plastic glue formula or glue on tissue paper. These make delightful mobiles and decorations.
4. Use a lid as the background for a mosaic of another media.
5. Some liquid soap bottle caps, such as those on liquid Ivory, are good for cutting shapes out of clay.
6. Trace around lids on a piece of paper, overlapping if desired, to make a design to color or paint (caterpillar, wheels, etc.)
7. Use lids for grease pencil boards.

MOIST TOWELETTE ORIGINALS

Students enjoy experimenting with a variety of media and moist towelettes to create original expressions of art for almost any occasion.

Materials Needed: moist towelettes, paint and brush, chalk, and crayons

Directions:

Experimenters try several ways (paint, chalk, crayons, marking pens, ink, beet juice, etc.) to apply color to towelettes at varying degrees of moistness. Some children may make flags and items for the flannel board while others depict holiday symbols, special events, characters, etc. on a towelette background.

OUTDOOR ART

Plan an art outing for one of the last colorful summer days. A class project is more fun than ever when nature is the classroom.

Materials Needed: tempera paint; brushes; string; materials from nature: a branch, small twigs and sticks, bark, leaves, pine cones, pebbles; various other media of any type

Preparation:

1. Before taking the walk, guide the students in discussing good items to bring back to the classroom.
2. Plan the art projects outside, if possible.

Directions:

The class takes a "nature walk" to gather suitable mobile materials (twigs, bark, leaves, cones, pebbles). If the day is conducive to working out of doors, they may paint their objects outside and suspend them by string from the branch (which may be painted or sprayed). If desired, students can make additional things for the branch: insects from pipe cleaners, caterpillars from clay, birds from styrofoam and feathers, etc.

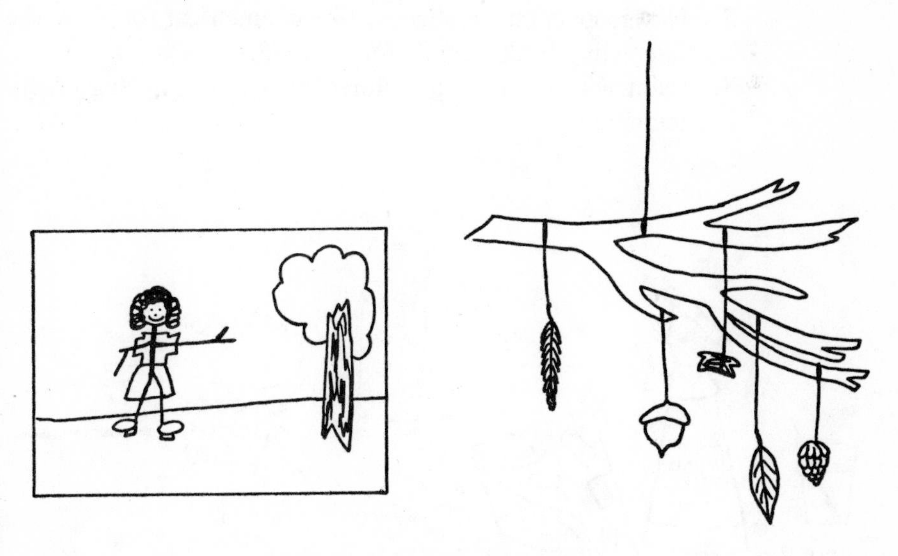

PAINTING EXPERIENCES

Challenge your students to discover ways of using unusual media and utensils in their art work. Who knows what might get their imaginations going?

Materials Needed: Roll-on deodorant bottles, shoe polish bottles, instant coffee, Q-tips, sponges, bottle caps, nails, liquid soap, tempera and anything else your imagination allows.

Directions:

Try out any of these possibilities:

1. Put paint in empty roll-on deodorant bottles and allow students to "roll on" the paint. Use bottles with removable ball holders, such as Dial and Fresh.
2. Put paint in empty liquid shoe polish bottles which have sponge applicators.
3. Instant coffee dissolved in water makes a different paint as does red cabbage juice, beet juice and food coloring.
4. Paint rocks outside on a nice day.
5. Mix Elmer's Glue or starch with paints. Cut-outs and lightweight objects stick to this paint mixture if they are applied before it is dry.
6. Q-Tips, sponges, bottle caps, and nails are also good substitutes for paint brushes.
7. Newspapers cut in shapes, like geometrical forms, make interesting backgrounds for painting.
8. Paint with liquid soap colored with food coloring or dry tempera.

PAINT WITH SHAVINGS

The teacher can use a mixture of paint and shavings to demonstrate how a common throw-away material can be used for a useful purpose.

Materials Needed: small containers, white glue, pencil sharpener shavings (or sawdust), paint, Popsicle sticks for stirring, cardboard or heavy paper, brushes, waxed paper (optional)

Directions:

Each student mixes pencil sharpener shavings with glue and paint until he has the desired spreading consistency. Experiment with the mixture to make a textured illustration. Children may paint numerals, letters, words, or shapes on cardboard; or, they may design three dimensional objects on waxed paper. Let the designs dry and then draw over them with a finger for kinesthetic experiences.

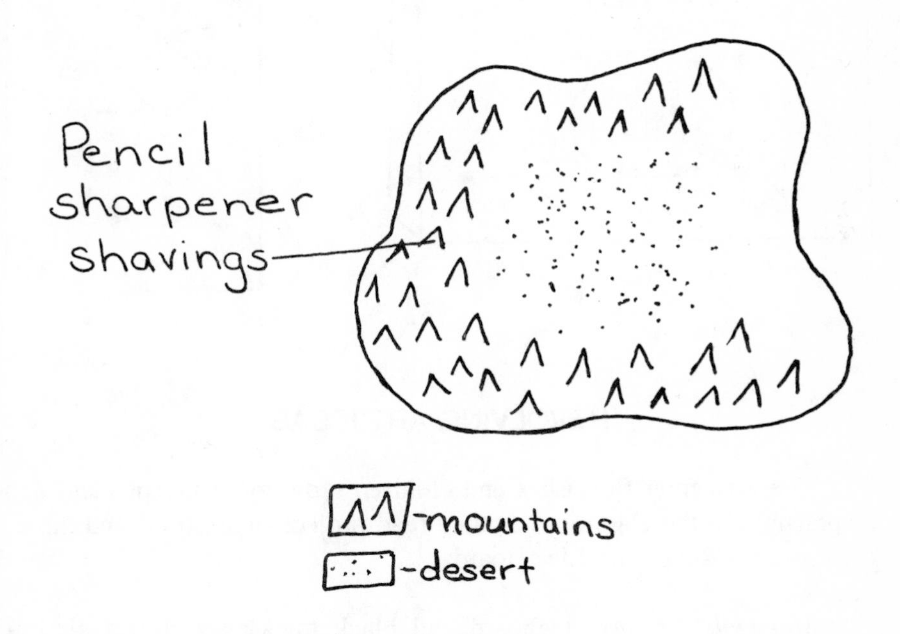

PHOTOGRAPHY ART

Students can produce imaginary photographs with a toy camera when they draw pictures that they have just taken. This is a great outdoor activity!

Materials Needed: boxes for making cameras (or toy cameras), scissors, paper, crayons

Directions:

Volunteers construct one or more cameras from boxes and other suitable materials. Class members can then view whatever people, objects, or scenes they wish to reproduce. Observing through this perspective allows students to focus on only one subject at a time. Completed photos can be arranged on a bulletin board entitled "Our Photos," "Shutter Bug Shots," or some other appropriate title.

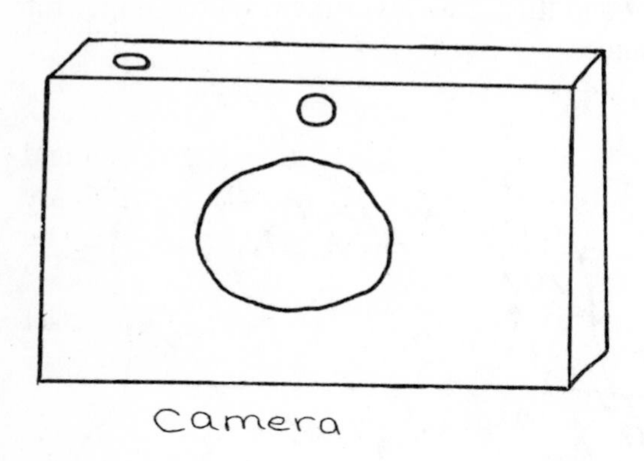

REVOLVING ART IDEAS

The art center flourishes and children grow more independent and responsible in the classroom as they read project suggestions and directions from a Revolving Idea Board.

Materials Needed: tagboard and black marking pens for six-by-twelve cards; tagboard or other material for display board with pockets, stapler, glue, two envelopes to store the cards.

Preparation:

1. Fashion a chart to hold the six-by-twelve title cards by stapling on four strips of tagboard 2½ inches wide and 13 inches long to form pockets.
2. Label one envelope "Fresh Art Ideas" and Label the other

"Used Art Ideas." At the beginning of the school year, place all the six-by-twelve cards in the "Fresh Art Ideas" envelope at the front of a file box or drawer and place the empty "Used Art Ideas" envelope at the back. After idea cards have been used for a few days in the chart, place them in the "Used" envelope for use at a later date.

3. To put the Revolving Idea Board into operation, choose about three idea cards and stand them in the pockets of the chart. In the fourth pocket, place a card that lists a "General" or "Freedom of Choice" item. Be certain to have all the necessary materials available in a central location so that students can help themselves to what they need.
4. Cut six-by-twelve inch card from tagboard and use a black marking pen to print a large idea title (like the one listed in this section) on each card. When printing on the cards, leave a three inch space at the bottom so they can stand in the chart. Cut 12 to 24 extra cards to be used as "General" and "Freedom of Choice" cards.

Here are a few ideas to get you started. Add to them and adapt these to your children's needs. The ideas with only general directions, like M, S, and T, listed below, may be placed on the "General" cards. "Freedom of Choice" cards may read "Create Anything You Wish," "Think of your Own Idea Today," "You and a Classmate May Make Up Your Own Project," etc.

A. Make something with buttons, beads, and pipe cleaners.
B. Draw and color an object on a piece of paper, cut it out and into puzzle pieces. Glue these onto a piece of construction paper, leaving a very narrow space between each piece to make an interesting puzzle picture.
C. Do a scribble drawing on a piece of newspaper that is cut into a triangle, a square, or any other shape.
D. Create a chalk and charcoal illustration.
E. Make a collage! Perhaps you can use natural materials—twigs, leaves, bark, weeds, etc.
F. Make something with rope or twine stiffened with wire or pipe cleaners.
G. Try a pearl tapioca design on black sandpaper, cardboard, or construction paper.
H. Use a small piece of carpet along with felt scraps to make a picture or design.

I. Illustrate a picture, glue it to cardboard, and cut it into a puzzle.
J. Use permanent marking pens on foil to make a picture or an abstract design.
K. Design something with drinking straws on construction paper.
L. Make a shadow box picture.
M. Make something from egg cartons.
N. Weave a design with two different-colored pieces of construction paper.
O. Create a felt design on a piece of burlap and hang it from a clothes hanger.
P. Use toothpicks and glue to make a toothpick sculpture.
Q. Make a ballpoint pen and/or pencil drawing.
R. Experiment by drawing with chalk on a moist towelette or damp paper.
S. Fold and decorate paper to look like whatever you please.
T. Use scraps to invent something that you have never seen before.
U. Use a sticker in a picture that you are making.
V. Draw a mural about a story, poem, or play that you have read. Perhaps a friend will help you!
W. Make a clown wearing a funny hat.
X. Make a picture with yarn, glue, and crayons.
Y. Make a design by tracing around a number of lids.
Z. Use two or three pieces of chenille to make a picture or an object.
a. See what you can make with scraps of wood.
b. Model something from clay. Perhaps you will want to write a story about what you make.
c. Make anything with fake fur.
d. Make an interesting picture or sculpture with macaroni and pipe cleaners.
e. Use a paper plate for the background of a scene.
f. Make a sculpture from various sizes of lids.
g. See what you can do with watermelon seeds.
h. Nut shells can be used in all sorts of things. See what you can do with them.

i. Mix up a batch of "play dough" to model.

   ½ cup salt
   1 cup flour
   ½ cup water
   Stir well in a bowl, knead with you hands, and model.

j. Try to make something with wood or plastic sticks.
k. Make an ecology poster.
l. Choose colorful scraps of paper and fabric to make a picture.
m. Use any type of media you desire to make a holiday picture.
n. Create a design using the letters in your name (or another word).
o. Make a picture using two to four reinforcement rings.
p. Design something from materials that are cut from a paper punch—paper, cardboard, plastic.
q. Make a picture from greeting cards or wrapping paper.
r. Make a personal mobile or chart using photos or illustration of yourself.
s. Make a pussy willow picture using puffed wheat.
t. Make a bunny from six paper eggs.
u. Create a scarecrow with straw, fabric, and whatever else you wish to use.
v. Make a picture using as many different materials as you can think of.
w. Help celebrate a holiday with a mobile made of holiday symbols.
x. Make a movable picture by cutting a slot in the background paper and moving a paper object up and down (or back and forth) in this slot.
y. Outline a foot and/or hand and make a design with it.
z. Sew a picture on a So-Sew/Mat (see Sew-So Kit in Chapter 11).

Directions:

Eager students read the four idea cards and select the ones that they want to try, either alone or with friends. They gather the necessary media and independently do the projects of their choice. The completed work may be displayed and discussed as desired. Even shy students are willing to relate what they "discovered" in working with certain media.

The three cards with specific directions can be changed about every week, while a "Freedom of Choice" or "General" card can remain longer.

When a student uses the last of a certain material needed for an activity, he may turn over that idea card, which both warns classmates not to begin that project and alerts the teacher that he either needs to replace those materials or exchange that card for another one.

Variation:

All art project ideas listed above can, of course, be enjoyed even if the Revolving Idea Board is not used.

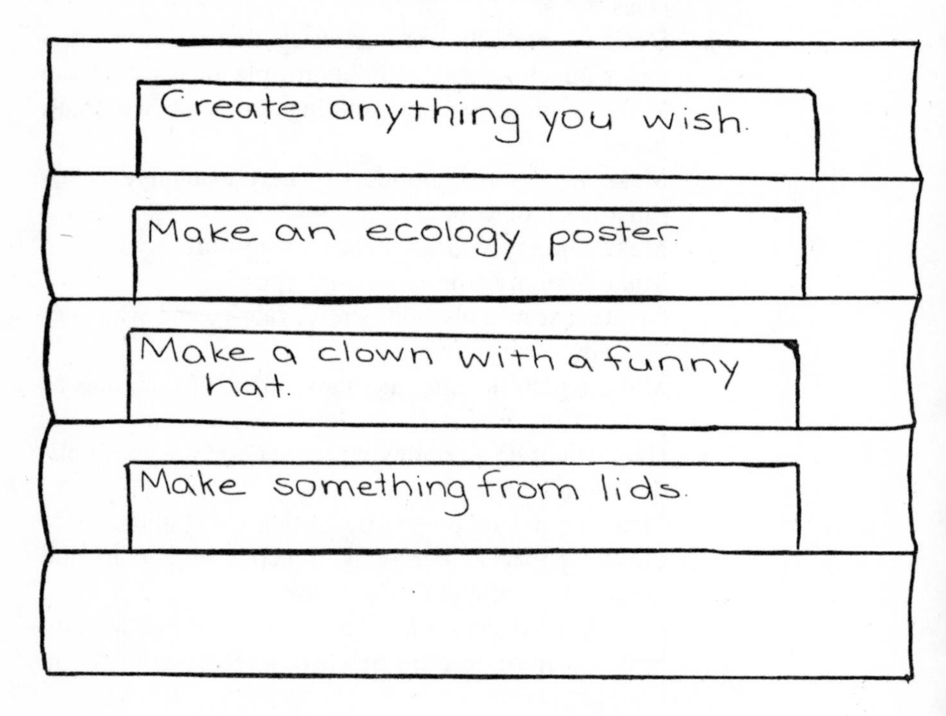

THREE DIMENSIONAL STAND-UPS

Three dimensional panoramas present children with the challenge of seeing a project develop through careful planning. By combining backgrounds and foregrounds, the children can create effective stand-up scenes for any occasion.

Materials Needed: construction paper—one sheet of nine x 12 inches for the background and one sheet of six x 18 inches for the foreground, scissors, glue, crayons or other coloring media of your choice

Directions:

Students adjust the width of their six x 18 inch foreground paper by creasing the sides, which will later be glued behind the background piece. For an authentic 3-D effect, plan to let this foreground stand out an inch (or even more) from the taller background; color or paint it to look like a fence (folded accordian-style), a brick or stone wall, a windowsill, etc. Or, the foreground paper can be illustrated with shrubs and bushes, a vehicle, animals, people, a fire hydrant, etc.

The background can be decorated to look like a skyline, a building, the sky, a windowpane and what is seen through it, etc.

Complete the panoramas by gluing the creased sides of the foregrounds to the backgrounds. These make nice displays for holidays or other special events.

TISSUE SCULPTURES

Facial tissues dipped in diluted glue provide a pliable medium for aspiring sculptures.

Materials Needed: durable facial tissues (or paper towels), white glue, bowls and measuring cups (or small throw away containers), newspapers, wax paper, paint (optional)

Preparation:

The teacher may prefer to mix the solution of equal parts of glue and water for younger students.

Directions:

To prepare for sculpting, the students cover tables with newspapers topped with wax paper and then mix their own glue solutions. Tissues are soaked in the solution for a few seconds, gently squeezed to eliminate excess fluid, and carefully unfolded—one at a time.

One group of students may wish to model an animal which is then glued onto a farmyard background. Another group may wish to cooperatively make a family of animals or people to be

attached to a park or zoo scene. Individuals may choose to place their sculptures in the art center for a classmate to paint or use in another project.

After the sculptures have dried overnight (or longer) on wax paper, they can be painted and mounted.

Variations:

1. The sculptures might be used to decorate the facial tissue box in the classroom or at home.
2. Sculptures can be hung as mobiles in connection with a unit, geometric figures, etc.

SPONGY DIMENSIONS

Once students are introduced to this three dimensional effect, they can experiment with all kinds of ways to use sponges for 3-D art projects.

Materials Needed: foam or sponge (sometimes used for packaging purposes), glue, construction paper, crayons, scissors, and other suitable media.

Directions:

Make two identical (or similar) pictures or designs from construction or other paper, cutting one slightly larger than the other. They may be done with crayons, paint, chalk, fabric, or anything else that is appealing. Glue a small piece of sponge on the back of the smaller cut-out, which will be in the foreground. Finish the project by gluing the sponge to the larger background piece.

Variation:
Make a three dimensional bulletin board picture or design as an interest group project.

STARCHY-PAINT CREATIONS

Students find it challenging, but rewarding, to arrange figures on an adhesive background. The activity involves careful planning and organization for a good design.

Materials Needed: tempera or finger paint, pencils, starch, paper, scissors

Preparation:
Use one part tempera or finger paint to one part liquid starch to make starchy-paint.

Directions:
Children draw and cut out scenes or designs which are placed on a starchy-paint background sheet before it dries; no glue is necessary. If desired, the picture can be pressed with heavy books when it is dry.

Chapter 10

Recycling into Crafts

A COLLECTOR'S PLAQUE

Each child becomes a collector of his favorite objects in this activity. A plaque for display encourages the younger students to classify and collect objects around them and the older students find it an ideal way to expand and exhibit their hobbies.

Materials Needed: pizza or cake plate (or cardboard box) for each collector, poptop lids for hangers (optional), other items such as magazines might be needed when children decide on their collections, small bulletin board or blackboard for posting "Items Wanted"

Directions:

To arouse interest and prompt classmates to collect items that fascinate them, students suggest possiblities for collections. As each student makes his decision, he receives a pizza plate or a box on which to place his first treasures. A board may be awarded when a student obtains five or six items. These may be decorated and hung on a wall or bulletin board where they will be available for additions. Students may trade or share items with others by posting "Items Wanted" information and exchanging at a specified time. Plaques can be shellacked (liquid or spray) to preserve them.

Students may think of collecting the following objects (the teacher can suggest ones not mentioned):

advertisements
autographs
baseball cards
butterflies
buttons
cartoons
decorative trim
fabric
flower seeds
fossils
greeting cards
leaves
matchbook covers
pen caps
pins
photos
playing cards
post cards
pop bottle caps
napkins
nutshells
seashells
tags
trinkets
valentines
vegetable and/or fruit seeds
wood from different trees
poems or riddles

pictures of all kinds about a particular subject: chairs only, all kinds of furniture, musical instruments, old cars, airplanes, professional football helmets.

Pictures might be overlapped on the plaque or be glued in an appealing arrangement.

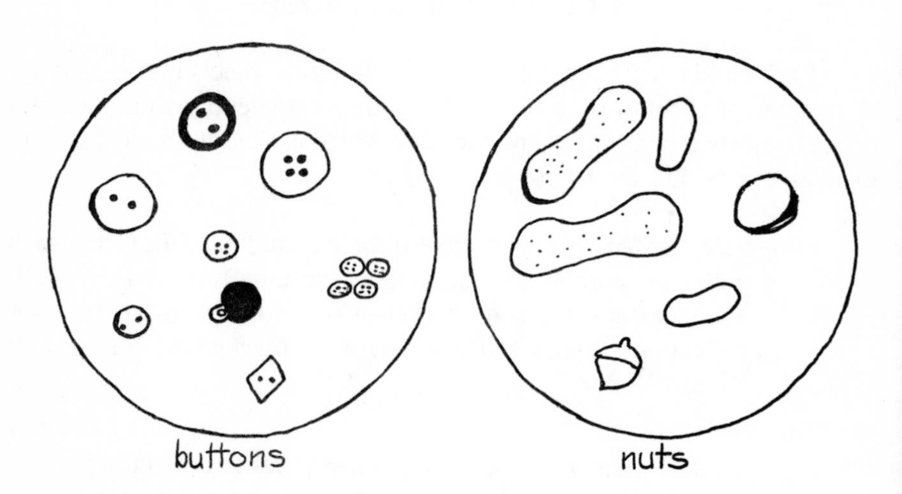

CANDY BAR CRAFTS

Candy Bar Crafts are fun any time, but especially on a party day when they can be used as favors and later eaten at snack time.

Materials Needed: candy bars of different shapes, scissors, crayons, glue, and some extras like tissue paper, construction paper scraps, pipe cleaners, buttons or plastic eyes, rick rack, decorative trim, curtain puffs (ball fringe), cotton puffs, yarn, felt, and other suitable items.

Directions:

After the students brainstorm to envision wrapped candy bars as animals, creatures, designs, vehicles, etc., they choose their favorite bars and decorate them to resemble other things.

The party fun continues as children admire their classmates' creations before the candy is either eaten or taken home for families to see and share.

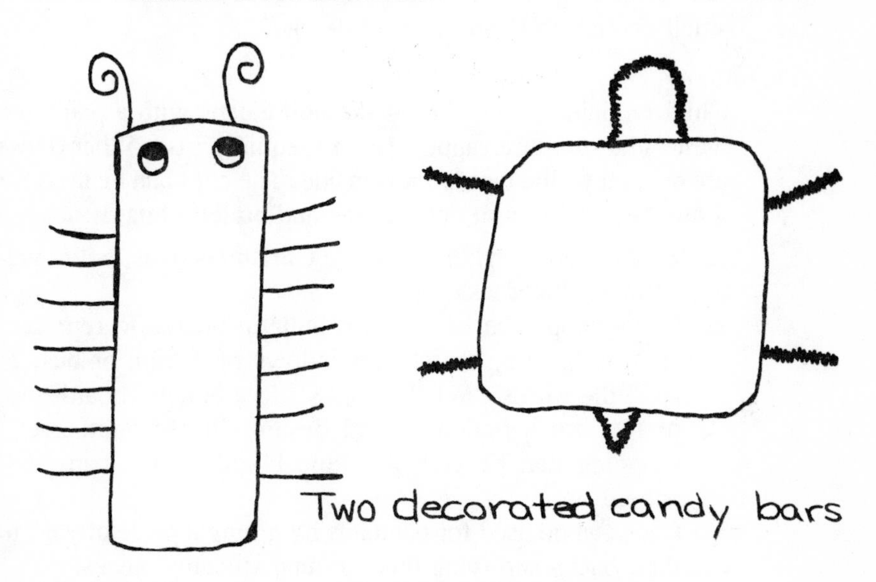

Two decorated candy bars

CRAFTS WITH BOTTLE CAPS

Since pop bottle caps are accessible to almost everyone, they are ideal for many practical, creative craft and art projects, including the ones that follow.

Hand Scraper for Shoes

Materials Needed: sandpaper, tempera or other paint, white glue, wood scraps (nearly any size and shape that children can easily hold in one hand to scrape dirty shoes), pop bottle caps, hammer and short nails (optional), shellac (liquid or spray) to cover paint

Directions:

Children sandpaper their piece of wood until it's smooth, paint the wood and let it dry, and apply shellac. (If spray shellac is used, the teacher or an older student may want to do it outside or in an area that is well ventilated and covered with newspapers.) When the shellac is dry, bottle caps are attached at one end and on only one side of the wood. At home or at school, the caps are pounded onto the wood, flat sides down, with one short nail.

Photo Caps

Materials Needed: pop bottle caps, photo of each child's face that is small enough to fit inside a bottle cap.

Directions:

Children paint the outside of the bottle caps with a paint and white glue mixture (approximately equal parts). When these are dry, they glue their photos inside. The caps can be used for a number of different decorations and bulletin boards:

1. Picture caps can help decorate Christmas trees, bells, valentines, shamrocks, etc.
2. Picture caps can be used on bulletin boards to represent children peering from the windows of a train or bus, to spell the words "WE" or "US" in a bulletin board title, or to form a bulletin board design. Pieces of magnetic stripping can be tacked to the board so the caps will adhere.
3. Caps can be used for pendants by gluing a piece of yarn to their backs and tying them around students' necks.

Variations:

Place bottle caps in the art center for collector's plaques, checkers, mosaics, collages, and for bottle cap and Popsicle stick sculpture. (Older students might like to use a pliers and a vise grip for this project.) Of course, caps can be utilized in many other ways that the students can imagine.

JAR RING PLAQUES

Unique plaques from discarded jar rings are exciting to produce and fun either to give as gifts or display at home or at school.

Materials Needed: jar rings, marking pens or a tempera-glue mixture, pencil, scissors, brushes, cardboard, glue, fabric or colored paper, items to decorate a picture: tiny flowers, shells, stones, felt, trimmings, scraps of wallpaper, etc.

Directions:

Color the rings with marking pens or a tempera-glue mixture. As they are drying, glue a scrap of fabric like felt or burlap (or paper) to a piece of cardboard that is at least as large as the jar ring. Lay the jar ring on top of this fabric-cardboard (or paper-cardboard) and mark very lightly with a pencil where the jar ring frame will be glued later. Now make your decoration for inside the ring and glue it to the fabric background. Glue the jar ring to the fabric (or paper), cut off the excess, let it dry, and hang it to enjoy as an art object.

Variation:

Decorate and glue a piece of paper between two colored rings for decorations to hang about a room or on the Christmas tree.

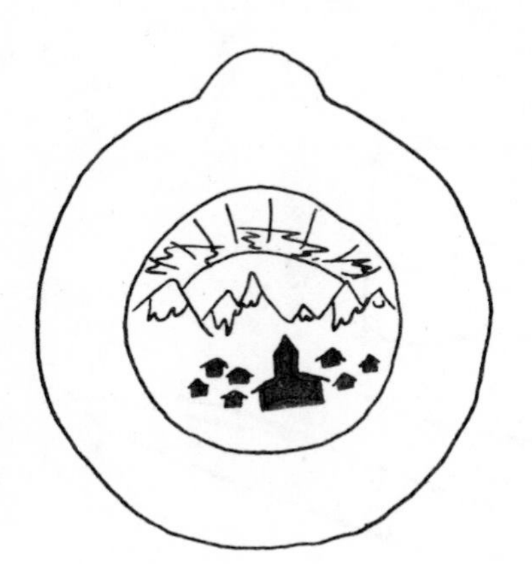

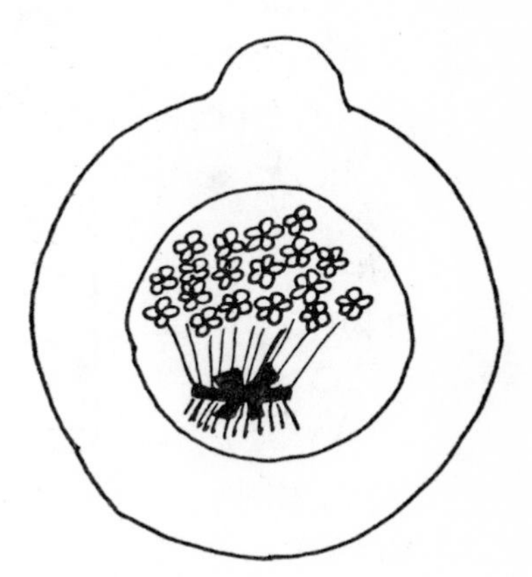

PEN OR PENCIL HOLDER

A clever pen or pencil holder can easily be made with two discarded lids and some plaster of Paris. Students enjoy making these for themselves or as gifts for relatives, class speakers, and student teachers.

Materials Needed: the top of a lipstick tube or a ballpoint pen cap; one spray can lid; plaster of Paris (or clay that will harden);

decorating materials like Contact paper scraps, rick rack, felt, tiny flowers, shells, or sewing trim; spray paint for plastic (optional)

Directions:

Mix plaster of Paris (equal parts plaster and water) and pour it into a spray can lid until the lid is about three-quarters full. When the plaster starts to harden (a very short time), place either a lipstick tube top or a ballpoint pen cap in the plaster at a slight slant, holding the cap until it will stand alone. Decorate the spray can lid with available materials and/or spray paint it.

Variations:

1. More than one lipstick tube top can be placed in the plaster of Paris to hold both a pen and a pencil.
2. A holder for scissors can be made in the same manner by placing the lipstick tube top in the plaster in a more upright position.

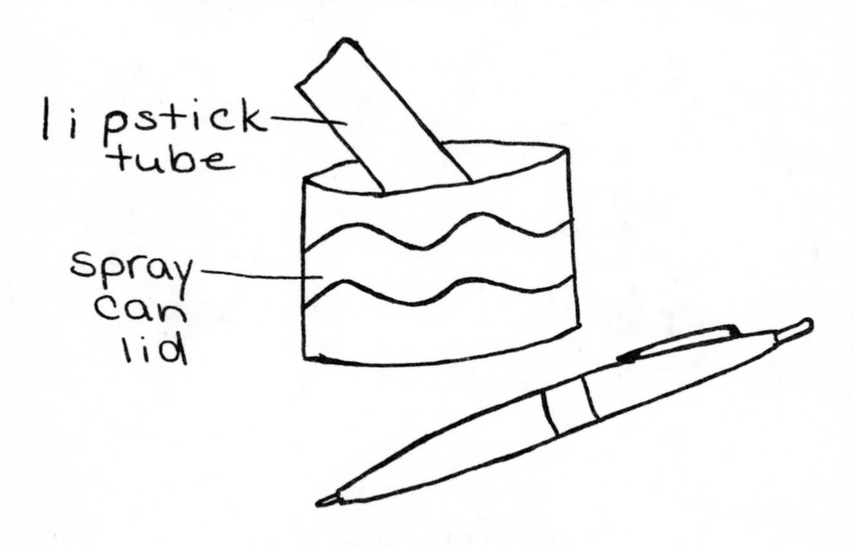

PLASTIC PUZZLES

Plastic lids from coffee cans and ice cream buckets double as great puzzle projects that children can solve at their desks or in the learning center.

Needed: students' original illustrations and/or magazine pictures, scissors, white glue, crayons, paper

Preparation:

Cut off the rims of the lids. The teacher may wish to make puzzles for the younger students.

Directions:

Project participants draw around the lids on either blank paper (to be colorfully illustrated) or on magazine pictures. These circular scenes are then glued to the lids and placed under heavy books to dry. Puzzles are formed by cutting the circles into pieces. Each puzzle can be held in a second lid, with a rim still on it, for storage.

Variation:

Laminate children's pictures before cutting them into puzzles.

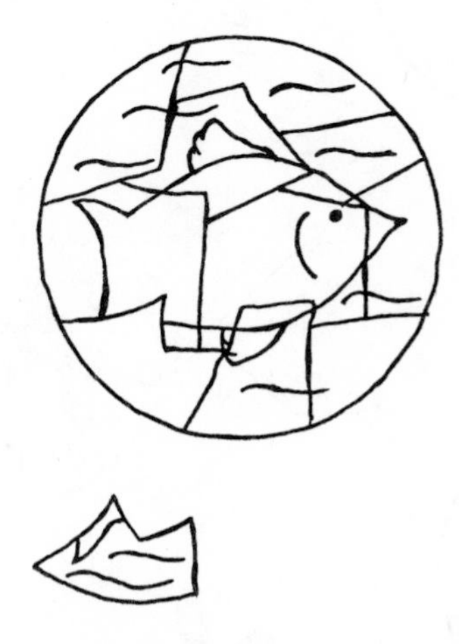

POM POM ANIMALS

These soft, cuddly pom pom animals are fun to make anytime, even at a party. The teacher may buy the materials with party money so that children can make them on the day of a party.

Materials Needed: scissors; at least two different sizes of pom poms made from yarn or purchased (cotton balls can be used); plastic eyes or small buttons; cardboard and/or felt for patterns; pipe cleaners for the rabbit; felt, beads, buttons, or some other material for noses, mouths, and other trim

Preparation:

The teacher will need to cut out the cardboard and/or felt back for young children.

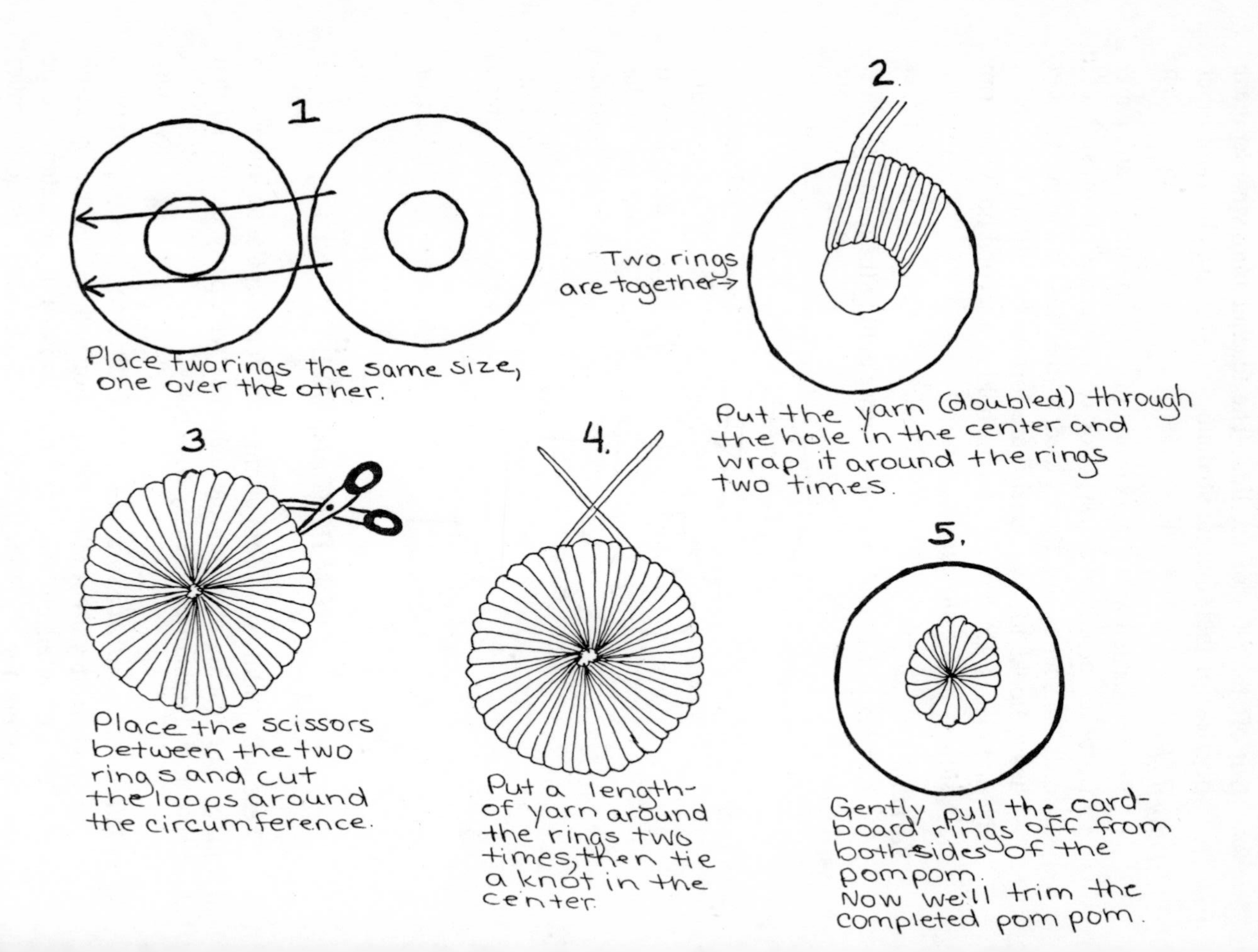
1
Place two rings the same size,
one over the other.
2.
Two rings
are together→
Put the yarn (doubled) through
the hole in the center and
wrap it around the rings
two times.
3
Place the scissors
between the two
rings and cut
the loops around
the circumference.
4.
Put a length-
of yarn around
the rings two
times, then tie
a knot in the
center.
5.
Gently pull the card-
board rings off from
both sides of the
pompom.
Now we'll trim the
completed pom pom.

Directions:

Glue large pom poms onto either a cardboard or felt form (or felt backed with cardboard) and add eyes, mouth, and other appropriate characteristics. Glue on smaller pom poms, which may be a different color than the large ones, for ears and paws. Pipe cleaners serve well as rabbit ears. The animals become children's pins or ornaments when backed with small safety pins or magnetic tape.

Jan Langemo worked out the directions for these pom poms:

A. Wind yarn tightly around a cardboard rectangle half as wide as the desired diameter of the finished pom pom (50-75 times for a pom pom 2 inches in diameter). Slip the yarn off the cardboard and tie it securely around the middle with a few inches of yarn. Cut and trim the loops.

B. Cut two pieces of cardboard like doughnuts (including a hole in the center) as large in diameter as the pom poms are to be. Wind double yarn around both rings, placed back to back until they are well filled. Holding the rings at the center, cut the loops around the outside of the rings. Slip a length of yarn in between the cardboard rings, let go of the center of the rings, and tie the length of yarn twice completely around the strands near the center of the rings. Gently pull off the rings and trim the pom pom.

Older children can make pom poms for younger children or assist the teacher in helping them.

Variations:

1. Use pom pom animals as manipulative aids for practice in counting and learning math facts.
2. Use the animals in bulletin board learning experiences. (Colors, comparatives like "bigger" and "smaller," the spelling of their names and colors)
3. Use small pom pom animals on the felt board.
4. Make pom pom animals to give as gifts.
5. Hang them on a Christmas tree.
6. Use several animals to make a zoo mobile.
7. The animals can be made from large pom poms that cheerleaders use.

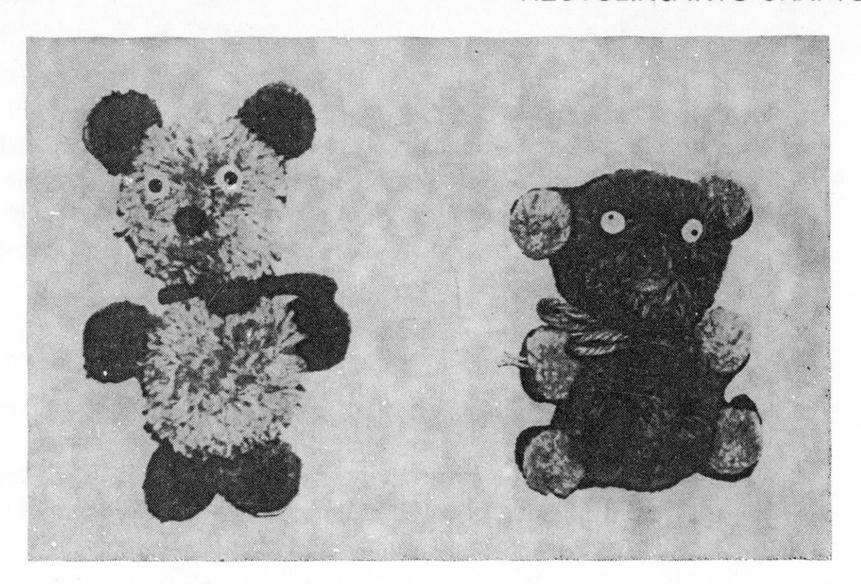

RECYCLED POTATO CHIP CANISTERS

Children can recycle potato chip canisters into many attractive and useful items.

Materials Needed: potato chip canisters (like those made by Pringles), glue, suitable materials to cover the canisters: wrap-

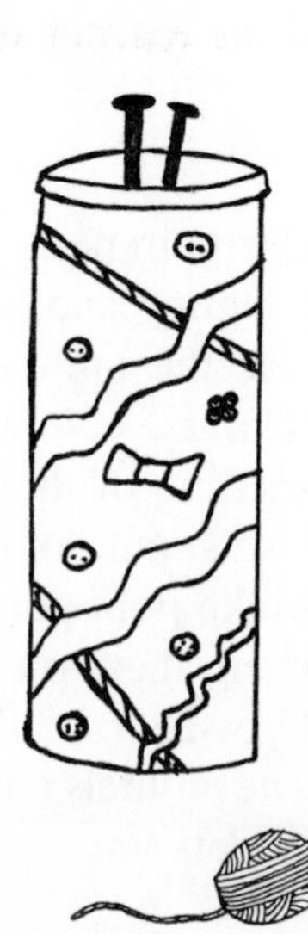

ping paper, wallpaper, pictures, Contact paper, fabric, greeting cards, carpet remnants, etc.

Directions:

The class lists together a number of ways to use a recycled potato chip canister. They cover their canisters with appropriate materials and use them for any of the following: combs and brushes, curlers and pins, kitchen equipment, knitting needles, notions, pencils, toys, rubber bands, small fishing equipment, string, etc.

SIT-ON-MAT

Each child has the experience of planning and completing an object that he can actually use when he constructs a sit-on-mat.

Materials Needed: transparent plastic bag large enough to sit on, paper punch or needle, yarn or cord, padding—newspapers, magazines, sponge, foam, newspaper wrapped in wallpaper, towel, scrap piece of carpet or some other suitable item

Directions:

The children each decorate the outside layer of newspaper or other padding with crayons, marking pens, or paints, and place the padding inside a large plastic bag. As they hold together the tops of the bags, punch holes (unless a needle is used) across the edge about two inches from the top and one half to one inch apart. (See illustration.) Lace or sew the tops with yarn (or other suitable material), leaving enough yarn for a shoulder strap.

The mat can be used for indoor story telling or on outings when the group stops for an ecological discussion, snack time, a rest during a nature walk, or an outdoor story time. (Stories with outdoor settings seem more meaningful when read outside of the classroom.)

SOAP BOTTLE VIEWER

"Show and Tell" can stimulate the curiosity of a class. In this version of "Show and Tell" classmates peer at each other's slide pictures through a soap bottle viewer.

Materials Needed: large translucent liquid soap container, cardboard or paper strips, small cards that will slide into the slot in the bottle, glue, pointed scissors, crayons

Slide Viewer Directions:

1. Cut a slot on one side near the bottom of a bottle so that a card can be slid in and out of it.
2. Cut cardboard pieces to fit in the slot.
3. Decorate the cards with pictures, numerals, alphabet letters, and/or designs and appropriate purchased stickers; glue these to the cardboard pieces.
4. See the completed slides by placing one at a time in the slot and pointing the viewer toward a light.

Filmstrip Viewer Directions:

1. Cut slots on opposite sides of a liquid soap bottle so that a strip of cardboard can be slid from one side to the other.

2. Create filmstrips by either drawing a sequence of illustrations on cardboard strips or by covering them with comic strips from newspapers, and magazines.

WATERING PITCHER

A plastic container with a handle can be transformed into a pitcher for watering plants at school or at home. Some of the students might like to make these practical pitchers for gifts to give on birthdays or holidays.

Materials Needed: sharp scissors (for teacher's use only) or other cutting tool, plastic fabric softener bottle or soap bottle with a handle on one side, glue, scraps of vinyl cloth, Contact paper, or any other material that can be used to make the containers more attractive

Preparation:

1. Wash out a plastic container and cut off its top. (The top can be kept and used as a funnel.)
2. On the opposite side from the handle, cut out a V-shape to make a spout.

Directions:

Decorate the pitcher with scraps of vinyl cloth or Contact paper. Older students can participate in the preparation.

Brainstorming to see how many things can be made from such a container encourages creative thinking, results in a vast storehouse of project ideas, and promotes ecology.

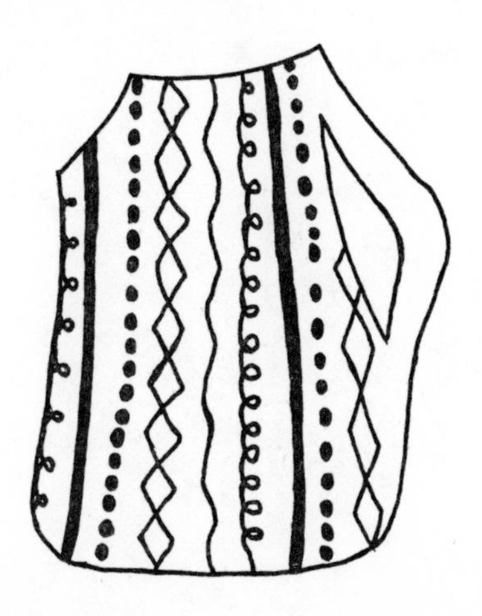

Chapter 11

Experiences in Cooking and Sewing

FOOD FOR THOUGHT

Students become very good thinkers when their thoughts are turned toward food. Occasionally, students are actually given a small amount of food that begins with a specific sound that they are studying.

Materials Needed: Occasionally needed is a small amount of food for each student that begins with the initial sound being studied. This may include consonants, vowels, digraphs, and blends.

Directions:

Students think of as many foods as possible that begin with a letter that the teacher prints on the experience chart or blackboard. For example, the teacher may print "B" on the chart. Students respond by naming bananas, beets, bologna, etc. If they do not suggest the following words, the teacher may.

Food for Thought

A.	apples, animal crackers, apricots
B.	bananas, blueberries, beans
C.	celery, carrots, cider, cocoa
D.	doughnuts, dill pickle, dates
E.	eggnog, egg, endive, éclair
F.	figs, fudge
G.	gingerbread, gum drops
H.	hash, ham pieces, Hershey Chocolate, honey
I.	ice cream, iced tea, instant pudding
J.	Jello, jelly, jelly beans
K.	Kix, kohlrabi, kosher dill pickles
L.	lollipops, lemonade, lettuce, lime, lemon
M.	marshmallows, M&M candy, muffins
N.	nuts, noodles, noodle soup, nectarines
O.	olives, Ovaltine, oatmeal, omelets
P.	parsley, popped corn, peanut butter, pineapple, pears
Q.	quail, quick breads, Quaker Oats
R.	raisins, raspberries, rice, ravioli
S.	sandwich, sugar cookies, soy beans, salt water taffy
T.	tangerines, tomatoes, toast
U.	upside down cake, unleavened bread
V.	vanilla pudding, vegetables
W.	waffles, watermelon, watercress
X.	Xmas cookies
Y.	yams, yeast breads, yellow beans, yellow cake
Z.	Zwieback, zucchini squash
CH.	cherries, chocolate chips, cheddar cheese
SH.	shoestring potatoes, sherbet, shortcake
TH.	thumbprint cookies
WH.	Wheaties, whipped cream, wholewheat bread
dr.	drop of honey, dried fruit, dry cereal
tr.	Trident gum, trout, Triscuits (crackers)
gr.	graham crackers, grapes
br.	bread, brown sugar
fr.	French fries, French toast, fresh fruit

Variations:

Older students may think of as many foods as possible that begin with the letters in the alphabet and put them in alphabetical order to make a food dictionary or an alphabetical recipe book.

DANDY CANDY

The anticipation of making and eating candy is exciting in itself, but when each child has the opportunity to make an individual amount, he may discover that these recipes are among his favorites.

Potato Candy (Individual Recipe)

Materials Needed:

Ingredients: mashed potatoes, powdered sugar, peanut butter, coconut

Utensils: small mixing bowls (plastic ones work well), mixing spoons, measuring spoons and cups, waxed paper

Preparation: Mash the potatoes

Directions:

1 tablespoon mashed potatoes
1 tablespoon powdered sugar
1 teaspoon peanut butter

Each child mixes these ingredients in his mixing bowl until they are blended well and the dough is smooth. They add enough coconut to make the candy thick and drop it by teaspoons onto waxed paper. Sampling may begin after the candy has chilled for half an hour.

Potato Candy

Cream Cheese Candy

(Partners work together and share the candy.)

Materials Needed:

Ingredients: powdered sugar, cream cheese, flavoring, food coloring

Utensils: candy mint molds that can be purchased in stores that sell cake decorations (optional), measuring cups and spoons, mixing bowls, waxed paper, pastry cutters or forks

Preparation: Let the cream cheese stand at room temperature until it softens.

Directions:

¾ cup powdered sugar (add more if needed)
1 oz. cream cheese
⅛ tsp. flavoring—mint, maple, raspberry
2 - 3 drops food coloring, if desired

These ingredients are for each two children who work together. Partners mix the ingredients as if making pie dough, using a pastry cutter or a fork to cut the cream cheese into the powdered sugar (works much better if the cheese is soft). When all the ingredients are well mixed, children form balls from the dough the size of marbles, roll them in sugar and either press each ball into a mold or model candy shapes. If children make molded candy, they should unmold them at once on waxed paper.

Cream Cheese Candy

PUNCHY PUNCHES (INDIVIDUAL RECIPES)

Students are enthusiastic about making these punchy recipes that help them develop skills in measuring solids and liquids in an informal situation.

Tangy Punch

Materials Needed:

Ingredients: water, two or three different kinds of Tang —orange, grape, grapefruit

Utensils: plastic glass or paper cups, measuring and mixing spoons

Directions:

Children mix two teaspoons of Tang in one glass of cold water. Here are some examples of measurements:

1 tsp. orange Tang + 1 tsp. grape Tang = 2 teaspoons
1½ tsp. one flavor Tang + ½ tsp. another flavor = 2 teaspoons

A Licorice Stick Drink (A Great Halloween Treat)

Materials Needed:

Ingredients: orange Kool-Aid (mixed), club soda, licorice sticks with hollow centers, ice cubes

Utensils: pitcher for Kool-Aid, measuring cups, long spoon to mix Kool-Aid, glasses or cups for mixing and drinking, small spoons for stirring

Preparation: Mix the Kool-Aid beforehand. Older children may wish to also do this part.

Directions:

½ cup orange Kool-Aid
¼ cup Club Soda

Each child uses the above measurements to mix the liquids in a glass or cup. Ice cubes may be added. A piece of licorice in each glass or cup serves as a straw.

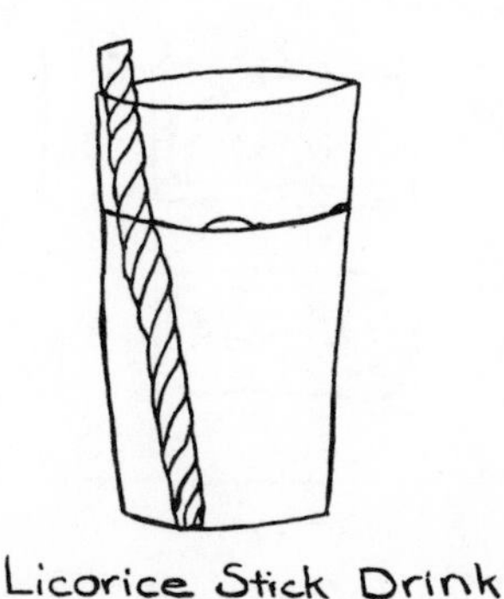

Licorice Stick Drink

SWEET AND SALTY CRACKERS

Budding chefs are thrilled with these tastebud tickling treats that are "just the thing" for a party or a snack. Almost as important as eating the results is the fact that children can *really* cook and decorate with these common ingredients.

Sweet Graham Cracker Treats
by Marcia Miller

Materials Needed:

Ingredients: graham crackers, brown sugar, margarine, walnuts or other nuts

Utensils: stove or electric oven and hot plate, mixing spoon, large shallow or cake or jelly roll pan, pancake turner

Preparation: Chop walnuts and preheat the oven to 350°.

Directions:

48 (1″x2″) graham crackers
1 cup brown sugar
1 cup (2 sticks) margarine
chopped walnuts

Place graham crackers in shallow baking pan. Melt brown sugar and margarine together and bring to a boil. Pour and spread the mixture over crackers. Sprinkle with chopped walnuts. Bake at 350° for 10 minutes, then let cool in pan for 5-10

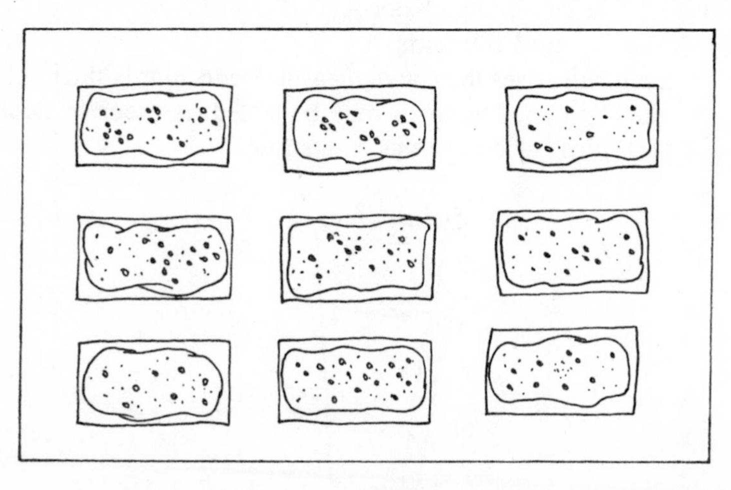

Sweet Graham Cracker Treats

minutes. Transfer to waxed paper with pancake turner until completely cooled.

Cheese and Salty Cracker Treats

Materials Needed:

Ingredients: soda or other salty crackers, cheese
Utensils: small cookie cutters, cheese slicer

Preparation: If cheese is unsliced, the teacher may wish to help younger children slice the cheese.

Directions:

On special days or any day children enjoy cutting out decorations from a slice of cheese with a cookie cutter and placing each on top of a soda cracker.

Variation:

Cold meat slices can be used instead of cheese (liverwurst, summer sausage, bologna, etc.).

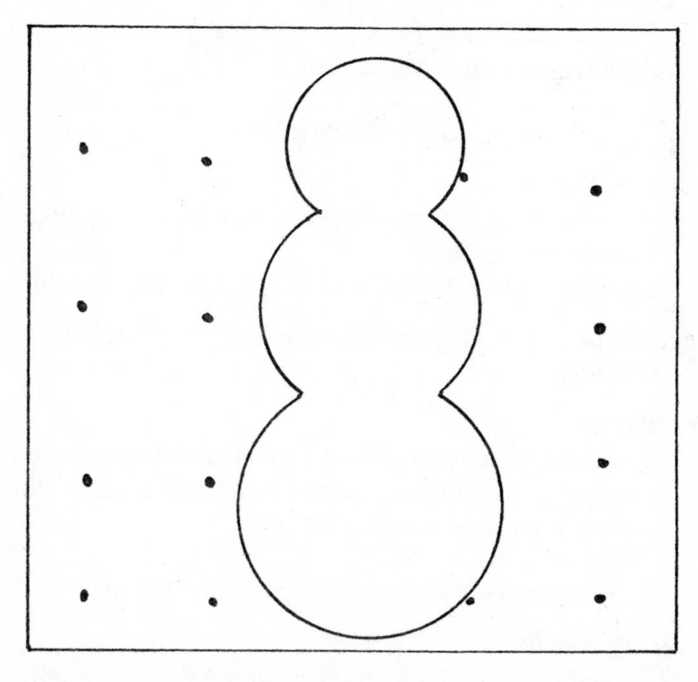

SWEET TREATS

These Sweet Treats will delight youngsters of all ages for they are easy to make and easy to eat!

Baked Caramel Corn

Materials Needed:

Ingredients: margarine, brown sugar, unsalted popcorn

Utensils: stove or hot plate and electric oven, small saucepan, popcorn popper, large mixing bowl and spoon, measuring cups, 2 shallow baking pans

Preparation: Pop enough corn to equal six quarts. Preheat oven to 350°.

Directions:

1 cup margarine (2 sticks)
1 cup firmly packed brown sugar
6 quarts unsalted popcorn

Melt butter and brown sugar together and add to the popped corn. Mix thoroughly. Spread in two shallow baking pans. Bake in 350° oven for eight minutes. Let cool in pan. Break caramel corn apart when cool.

Cake Sandwiches

Materials Needed:

Ingredients: gingerbread cake mix, whipped topping, pudding (instant or prepared)

Utensils: jelly roll pan, knives for spreading frosting

Preparation: Bake gingerbread cake mix in jellyroll pan and cool completely.

Directions:

Cut cake in squares. Make instant pudding (or use prepared pudding) and spread it between each square. Frost with whipped topping. Chill. Eat!

Dessert-A-B-C Special (Individual Recipe)

Materials Needed:

Ingredients: graham cracker or cornflake crumbs, cream cheese, powdered sugar, whipped topping (such as Cool Whip), prepared pudding for each child

Utensils: a transparent (or paper) cup and a small mixing bowl and spoon for each child, measuring spoons and cups, refrigerator space

Preparation:

1. Let the cream cheese stand at room temperature until soft.
2. Crush the graham crackers or cornflakes (or use prepared crumbs).
3. Mix the instant pudding with milk in a mixer if a prepared pudding isn't used. (Eight children can share one small box of instant pudding mixed with 2 cups of milk.)

Directions:

Each student mixes the following in his bowl (a throw-away plastic container works well) and layers it in a transparent plastic cup so he can see the different layers.

Layer A:

Place 1 tablespoon of graham cracker or cornflake crumbs in the bottom of the cup.

Layer B:

Mix together 1 ounce (oz.) softened cream cheese, 2 level tablespoons powdered sugar, and 2 heaping tablespoons whipped topping. Spread this mixture on Layer "A" and chill one-half to one hour.

Layer C:

Spread ¼ cup prepared or instant (see "Preparation") pudding of any flavor over Layer "B" (frozen prepared pudding can be thawed before measuring). Chill, then eat.

A-B-C Dessert

Pull needle to front side. Push needle back through from 1/8 inch behind to 1/8 inch ahead of first stitch.

French
Knot

Pull needle to front side, wind thread around point 3 times, push needle back through while holding knot in place.

Daisy
Stitch

Pull needle to front side, form a loop under point of needle, fasten loop with a small stitch at center.

Stitch diagonal lines across a row. Stitch lines slanting the opposite direction across the row.

Stitch several straight lines. Fasten them at center with 2 vertical stitches.

Blanket
Stitch

Pull needle to front side, form a loop with each stitch.

STITCHES CHART

When a chart illustrating a number of stitches is made available to a class, some students delight in learning how to do all of them. These people are usually pleased when asked to help classmates who need assistance with their sewing projects.

Materials Needed: tracing paper; pencils; tagboard; scissors; marking pen; directions (see "Preparation" and illustrations); needles; yarn, embroidery floss; fabric, vinyl cloth, fiberglass screen, foam, and other suitable material on which to practice stitches.

Preparation:

Trace the illustrations from the following chart and transfer them to a wall chart. (Older students can help make a chart.)

Directions:

The chart serves as a guide for children to experiment and practice stitches with any of the materials listed above. Projects may be attempted when children feel confident in doing a few stitches (perhaps as few as two for young students).

Variations:

1. Duplicate student copies like the wall chart so the directions can be taken home or used outside on a nice day. Some teachers may wish to use student copies instead of a wall chart.
2. Some of the older stitchery students may be interested in making a booklet of illustrated stitches, beginning with a copy their teacher gives them. Classmates can exchange stitches that they have improvised and adopt others from sewing books, mothers, grandmothers, etc.

AUTOGRAPH, PLEASE

The schoolroom becomes home when class members display their portraits on a large felt wall hanging. Each child personalizes his photo by sewing his autograph below it. Throughout the year the wall hanging can be displayed elsewhere in the school for special occasions and then left as a keepsake for the teacher.

Materials Needed: a large piece of felt, burlap, interfacing (washable), or any other material suitable for a wall hanging; a photo of each child; white glue; embroidery floss in several colors; thimble (optional); needle; a dowel slightly longer than the width of the fabric; yarn or cord; pencil; trim—ball fringe, appliques, etc. (optional)

Preparation:

1. Make a hem on the back of the felt at the top by turning back at least three-quarters inch of the material and sewing or gluing it in place. Check to see that the dowel will fit in this hem.
2. Use a pencil to draw lines on the felt where the children will sew their names, leaving enough space above each line to mount a picture.

Directions:

Each child prints his name on a line and sews over it with embroidery floss (see the sewing chart of stitches in this chapter for specific directions). A friend may do the sewing for a student who doesn't care to sew.

The children may help glue on the photos and add any desired trim. They slip the dowel into the hem and tie a length (12-24 inches) of yarn or cord to each end of the dowel, leaving enough slack in the cord to hang it from a hook.

Variations:

All kinds of pictures and designs for a wall hanging can be done as a class project.

1. A handkerchief or a scarf can be autographed as a keepsake for a student teacher or child who is leaving.
2. Children who are interested in making these hangings for gifts can each autograph his own small portrait wall hanging and add appropriate trim.

BUTTON, BUTTON, SEW ON A BUTTON

Sewing as many buttons on a numeral as the symbol indicates helps students to strengthen both sewing skills and mathematical concepts. This is an ideal manipulative aid for an activity center.

Materials Needed: buttons (for example: large blue buttons for tens and small red buttons for ones—you may choose to use the same color buttons that your math book uses to show the tens and ones columns), thread, needles, fabric (such as felt), scissors, thimbles, pencils.

Preparation:

Trace and cut out felt numerals for younger children and special education children; older children may assist in the preparation. Make available the buttons as suggested above.

Directions:

At a student's discretion, he may sew as many buttons on a fabric numeral as the number indicates. After this is completed, he glues the fabric numeral to a piece of tagboard, cuts it out, and either pins it on a bulletin board or tapes it to a wall to make an attractive and meaningful display.

Variation:

Young students and students in special education enjoy sewing various colored buttons to the same color fabric to make a collage with all sizes and shapes of buttons

SCREEN STITCHERY

Contrary to what its name implies, fiberglass screen does not have sharp edges. Children can safely use it to sew whatever fascinating pictures and abstract designs their imaginations can envision.

Materials Needed: a "Stitches Chart" (see "Stitches Chart" in this section), fiberglass screen, embroidery floss, needles, scissors, embroidery hoop (optional)

Preparation:

1. The teacher may make a large chart and/or duplicate student copies of the "Stitches Chart" found in this chapter.
2. Cut the fiberglass screen into whatever shapes and sizes the students want (older students may help or even cut their own).

Directions:

Stitchery students may follow directions on the chart or improvise stitches to sew whatever they wish on the screen. Some may choose to mark their sewing plan on the screen before beginning. Completed projects may be mounted and/or framed.

Variation:

Small children like to sew with a blunt needle and yarn on mesh vegetable and fruit sacks.

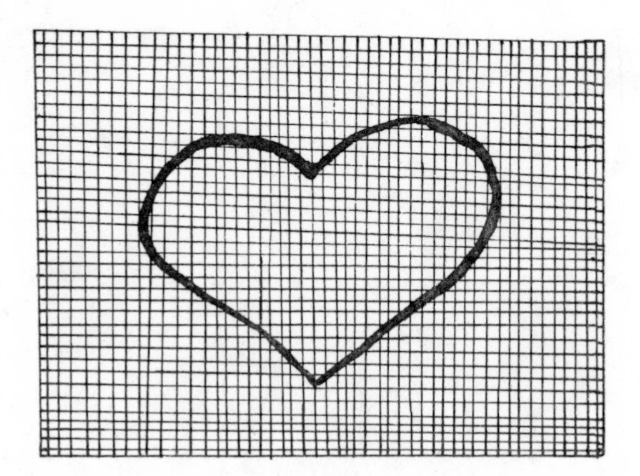

SEW WITH VINYL CLOTH

Vinyl cloth works well as a medium for sewing stuffed toys (such as the turtle described on p. 189), for abstract designs, and for stitching on a pattern outline that is printed on the vinyl cloth.

Materials Needed: vinyl cloth (available in most variety and fabric stores); thread, yarn or embroidery floss; needles; thimbles; discarded nylon hose, cotton batting, polyester filling, or other suitable material for stuffing; thin paper for tracing; pencils, scissors; pattern on the following page; crayons.

Preparation:

Trace the turtle pattern at the end of this section and transfer it to tagboard to make patterns for students. Younger students will enjoy turtles made by the teacher or by older students.

Directions:

Students draw around the turtle patterns on the back of vinyl cloth and cut them out. To insure balanced proportions, some stuffing can be done when half the sewing is completed, and then finished before the last few inches are stitched together. Each turtle becomes unique as the children add facial features with crayons either before or after the sewing.

A class can incorporate their new pets into group and individual activities by naming the turtles, writing about them, using them in plays or puppet shows, and inventing turtle games. Other vinyl cloth creations can include flowers for

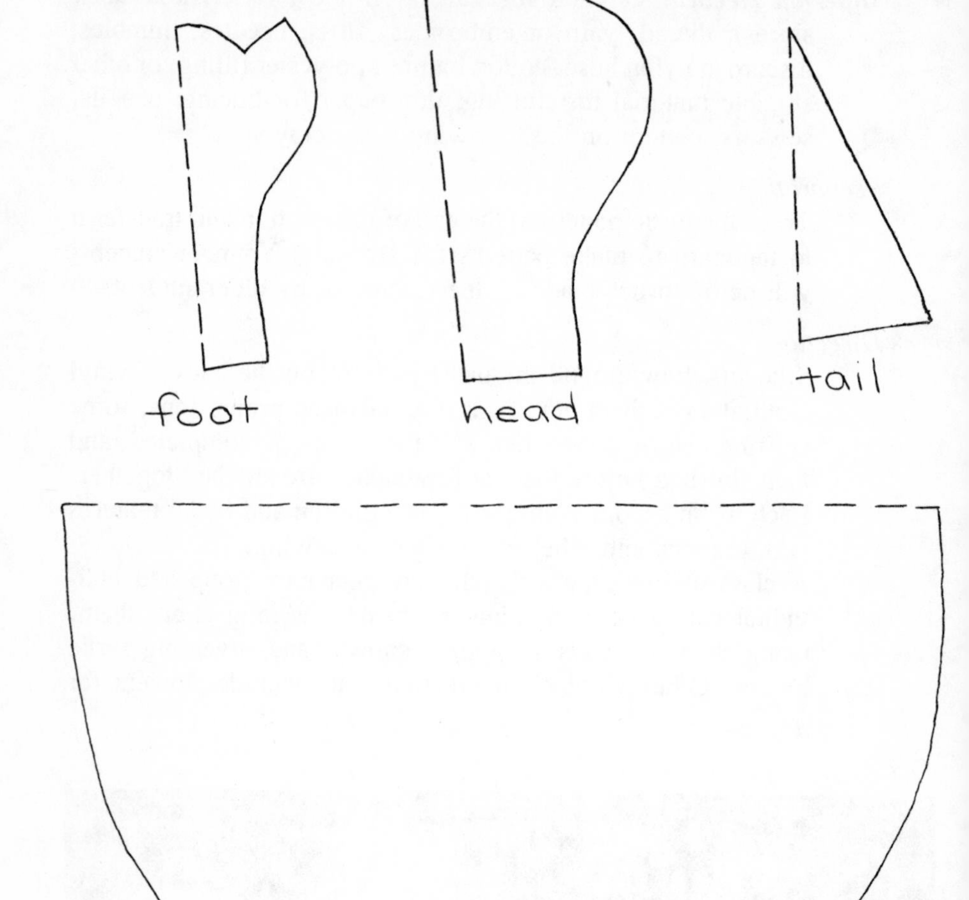

plaques, stuffed animals, large bulletin board items, and beanbags.

Variation:

Older students may wish to make a large hassock turtle (or

other animal) for classroom use or to give as a gift to the library, a primary class, or a hospital pediatrics ward. They can divide into committees and enlarge the small turtle (or other) pattern by using either one-quarter inch and one inch graph paper or a transparency on an overhead projector. Use the enlarged paper pattern to cut out vinyl cloth turtle and sew it with yarn as shown in illustration. Plastic eyes or buttons can be sewn on the head for the turtle's eyes and it can be stuffed with a styrofoam cushion. It can be gift wrapped with paper designed by the children, if desired. The entire class may present the gift, with a student-made card, if desired.

SO-SEW KIT

Stitchery students can learn and reinforce creative sewing skills with the individual or classroom So-Sew Kits, which include fabric, needles, thread, illustrated stitch directions, and ideas for variations. Kits can be purchased from:

Paul S. Amidon & Associates, Inc.
4329 Nicollet Avenue South
Minneapolis, MN 55417

Chapter 12

Bulletin Boards on Display

ARE YOU READY FOR SCHOOL? WE ARE!

Here is an easily-and quickly-made bulletin board for those busy days prior to the opening of school. New students are delighted to be greeted by these familiar smiling faces!

Materials Needed: yellow paper plates for smiling faces (sometimes plates or stationary with smiling faces can be purchased), yellow paper, black marking pen, pins, black background paper

Preparation:

1. Write the title on a piece of yellow paper with a marking pen.
2. Draw smiling faces on the plates, making them all look exactly alike.
3. Put up all of the materials (see illustration).

Directions:

During one of the first days of school (perhaps whenever students first mention it), the teacher and class may discuss the fact that all of the faces look alike. If someone doesn't make a statement about the problems there might be if *we all* looked

alike, the teacher can bring up the topic. With some thought and discussion, most students quickly realize that variety makes people, and life, more interesting.

The discussion may stimulate some children to write stories about the identical faces on the board. Later in the week, students may enjoy adding yarn hair, hats, freckles, hair ribbons, ears, etc. to the faces so that they, like people, are all different from each other.

Variation:

Other titles might be "Welcome Back To School," "Welcome, We're Glad You're Back, Too."

AQUARIUM MURAL

When children cooperate in creating an aquarium mural, they learn firsthand about organization and communication as well as experiencing the fun of observing marine life and drawing on these observations in their art-work.

Materials Needed: finger paint paper cut the desired size for the mural, finger paint (other paint can be used) thickened with liquid starch, crayons, scissors, clear plastic (optional)

Directions:

If possible, observe and discuss various kinds of fish in an aquarium. Children form groups and assign tasks (perhaps with the help of the teacher). They design, cut out, and organize pictures of marine life which may be laid aside while the background is painted (or some children paint while others make things). While the paint-starch mixture is still wet, the plants and fish are placed on the mural. If the mural wrinkles as it dries, its back may be pressed with heavy books or a warm iron. If desired, students can place clear plastic over the scene to represent the acquarium's glass. They may make a frame by outlining the bottom and sides with wide strips of black paper, extending the sides (at the top) above the imaginary water.

Variation:

An individual aquarium can be designed by each student, if desired.

BULLETIN BOARD DOG

The song title "Give the Dog a Bone" doubles as a catchy theme for a versatile bulletin board. Children are anxious to provide creative writing when it can be done on a paper bone for a lop-eared bulletin board dog.

Materials Needed: one large square of burlap (or paper) for a dog; several small pieces of fabric for facial features; paper cut in the shape of large bones; paper, cotton batting, or discarded nylon hose, etc. to stuff the nose; paper or fabric for the background; pins; letters for the title

Preparation:

1. Put up the background paper and letters.
2. Construct a large dog from burlap or other suitable material by following the easy directions below. A small group of older students can do this independently.
3. The teacher and students can cut paper to resemble large bones. If desired, lined writing paper can be used, which may be mounted on slightly larger construction paper bones.

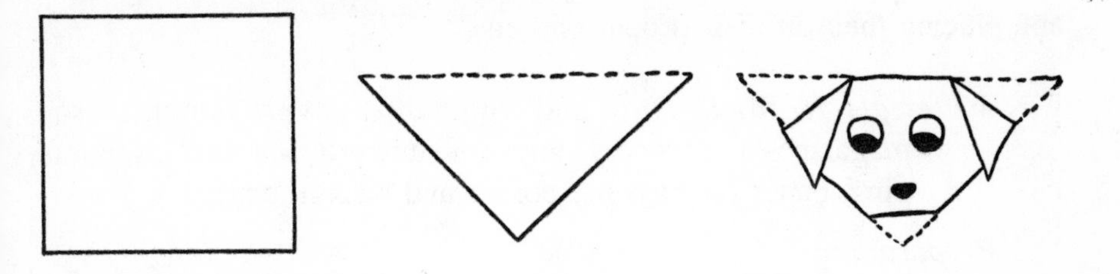

Directions:

Children find it fun to "Give the Dog a Bone" by writing poems and stories about dogs on bone-shaped paper. After each bone is completed, it is pinned near the bulletin board dog where everyone can read its inscription.

Variation:

This dog can be used for subjects other than creative writing—math, phonics, reading, spelling, etc.

FILL GOOD FOOD BASKETS

Students are directly involved in constructing this bulletin board because they have the responsibility of cutting out the fruit and vegetables and placing them in their proper baskets.

Materials Needed: fruit and vegetable advertisements from magazines and grocery stores (or student-made food), scissors, pins, paper for baskets, border and background

Preparation:

1. Obtain pictures of fruits and vegetables from magazines and/or produce managers in grocery stores.
2. Make two large baskets like the illustration below or by weaving paper strips. Print "Fruit" on one basket and "Vegetables" on the other.
3. Place the baskets on background paper on a bulletin board.

Directions:

Younger students cut fruit and vegetables from the advertisements and place each one in the proper basket.

Upper grade children can cut out foods for each of the four basic groups and make a food wheel.

Variations:

These paper fruits and vegetables can be arranged for a "still

life'' picture or cut in half to stimulate drawing. Only one-half of the fruit or vegetable is glued to white paper; an art student draws and uses appropriate coloring to make the picture look like a whole fruit or vegetable.

HERE COME THE CLOWNS

Nearly everyone is eager to create an original character and write about him when the teacher suggests making large balloon-carrying clowns to parade on a corridor wall.

Materials Needed: large sheets of colorful construction paper, scraps of fabric and yarn, buttons, masking tape (optional), penmanship paper (optional)

Directions:

The students make colorful clowns holding balloons on strings from a combination of the above (or other) media. Stories about the clowns can be written either directly on the balloons or on penmanship paper fastened to them. Clowns join the

hallway parade when their backs are stuck to the wall with pieces of rolled masking tape.

INDIVIDUAL BULLETIN BOARDS

Children experience a special pride in their work and learn to appreciate the work of others as they display specimens of completed assignments on individual bulletin boards.

Materials Needed: insulation board (also called fiberboard) for a number of bulletin boards, wide plastic tape, stick pins or tacks (Tac-Stick is safer for the young children)

Preparation:

Set aside a certain area in the classroom for the individual bulletin boards.

Directions:

Children can make bulletin boards (younger students with the help of a teacher or an older student) by framing fiberboard with wide plastic tape.

Participants may pin or tack work from any subject on their own bulletin boards and decorate them appropriately as desired.

The teacher may encourage children to change the displays often.

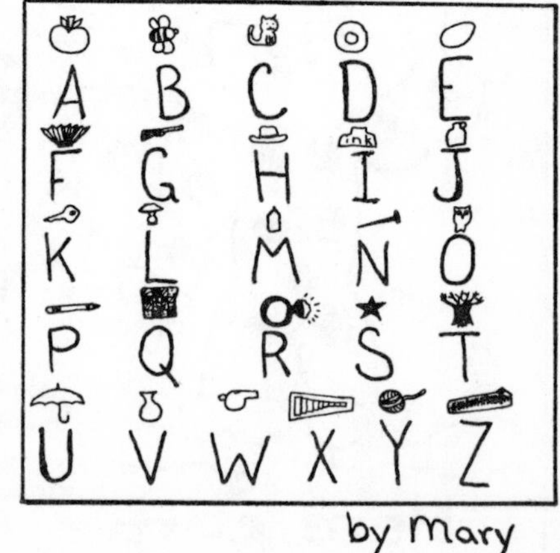

MY FAVORITE PROJECT

Original ideas in all subject areas are provided for a unique exhibit when students are encouraged to pursue special interest projects.

Materials Needed: Each student lists for the teacher the materials that he will need for his project if they are not available in one of the centers. As work on the projects proceeds, students may need to list materials that need replenishing.

Directions:

Before starting this activity, students and teachers discuss media potential and project possibilities. Suggestions might include: science experiments, mathematical aids or games, puppets and puppet show scripts, plays, original stories, poetry, scrapbooks, sewing projects, ecology posters, radio script on a tape recorder, art and craft items, etc. Each child completes a project and places it on a bulletin board or display table. The class may set aside time (and even invite parents or another class) to demonstrate certain projects like experiments, games, plays, etc.

OUTLINE GOOD BOOKS

Filling the outline of a seasonal symbol with their own illustrated book covers encourages children to read more library books. Book titles and themes are shared with classmates, as students view each other's work on a colorful bulletin board.

Materials Needed: materials to outline such as decorating chains, boat rope, Christmas rope, and any other suitable material; background and border paper; several colors of paper for book covers; pins

Preparation:

1. Make book covers by cutting paper twice as wide and as high as the desired cover size. Fold these sheets in half to look like book covers and place them in a box near a bulletin board.
2. Put up the bulletin board background and border.
3. Make a seasonal outline (turkey, heart, egg, etc.) on the bulletin board from boat rope, decorating chain, or other suitable medium. Older students gladly help with the preparation.

Directions:

When a student reads a book, he prints the title on the book cover, illustrates a picture on the front and/or inside it, and pins the cover on the bulletin board inside the outline. Each student reads as many books as possible to fill the outline.

Variation:

Older students may write a brief report inside the books.

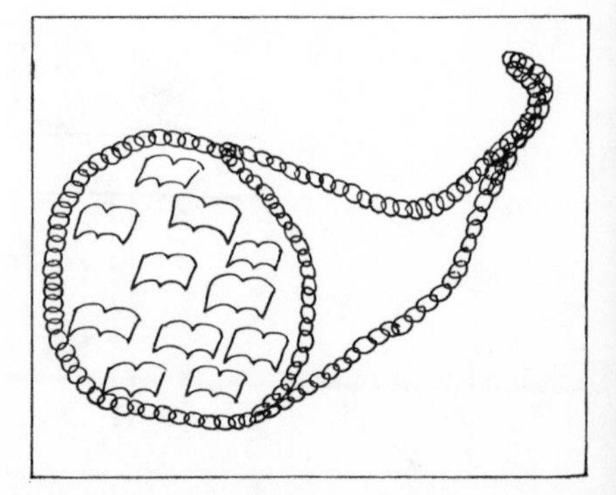

POM POM BOARDS

Making large pom pom animals for primary children to use is a worthy, yet challenging, art project for older students. When these beautiful visual aids are attached to a bulletin board, they can hold the attention of young children as their teacher guides them through various subject skills. For example, "The Three Bears" can be used to reinforce the word "three" and review the concept of a set of "three" in the following activity.

Materials Needed: see materials and directions for making pom poms under "Pom Pom Animals" in Chapter ten (make larger rings for these large animal pom poms). Additional materials include background paper, border, construction paper, glue, scissors, crayons, scraps of fabrics, woodgrain Contact paper for the table (or brown paper), and any other suitable materials students suggest.

Preparation:

1. A cooperating upper grade and primary teacher make plans for "The Three Bears" activity or another type of pom pom board.
2. Put up the background, a Contact-covered cardboard table and the three bears.

Directions:

Primary students discuss with their teacher the word "three" and tell which sets of "three" objects the bears on the bulletin board need. The students might volunteer to make three of each of the objects named—chairs, stairs, pillows, bowls, spoons, knives, forks, water glasses, etc.—to pin on the bulletin board.

WHAT'S HAPPENING IN ECOLOGY?

Youngsters become more aware of current news events when they are asked to find and display materials relating to a timely topic. Focusing their attention on local, state, and national happenings in ecology may be a good way to begin.

Materials Needed: current newspapers and news magazines, scissors, letters, pins or staples, old newspapers for background, red or black construction paper to be used both as a border and to back each picture and article displayed

Preparation:

1. Cover the bulletin board with a newspaper background. Add a red or black border and the title.
2. Both teacher and students may provide current newspapers and news magazines.
3. A box of red or black background paper should be accessible to the class so that each student can fasten his articles or pictures to a small background sheet before placing it on the bulletin board.

Directions:

Students use the current publications to locate and cut out articles and pictures. These clippings are then mounted on the red or black background paper and fastened to the bulletin board for others to see. Class or group discussions about some of the items may occur as time and interest allow.

Variations:

1. The students can be divided into three groups, with each group searching for information in one area. Group L finds local ecology news, S finds state, and N finds national.
2. Articles may be classified under the titles "Air Ecology," "Water Ecology," "Land Ecology."

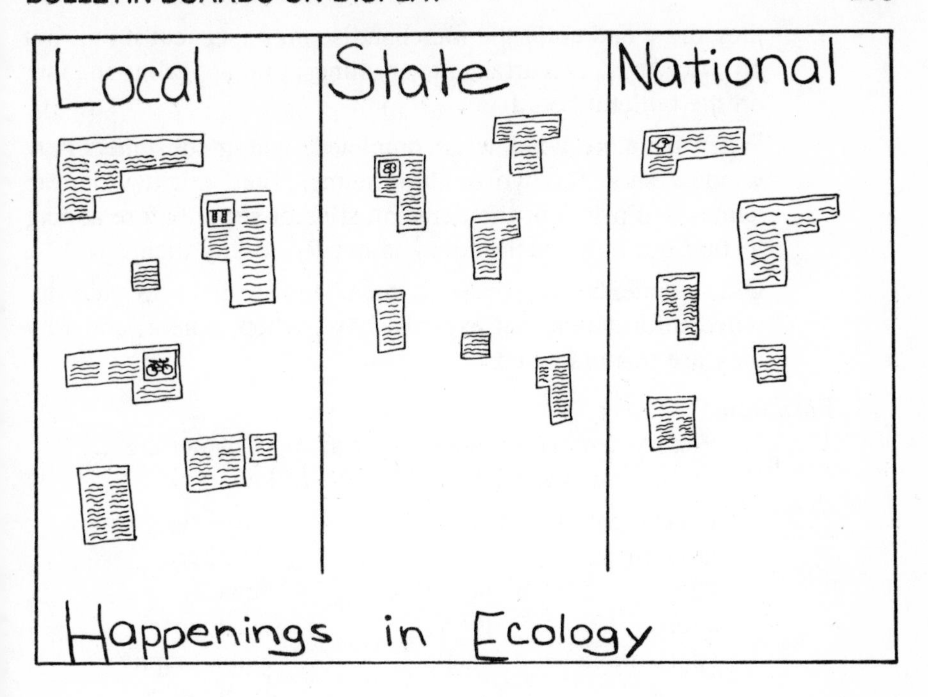

WINDOW SHOPPING ACTIVITIES

A bulletin board that resembles a vacant store window beckons students to fill it with merchandise that they create, price, and purchase. This fun activity from the adult world provides creative art experiences, strengthens concepts involving money, and passes along practical information about the merchandise involved.

Preparation:

1. Put up the background and the outline of a window on the bulletin board (see example).
2. One way students may choose the type of store display they wish to simulate is by voting for one out of three —such as a bakery, music shop, or shoestore.
3. When students have finished their pictures of merchandise, print the words that name the merchandise on slips of Manila paper and place them near the items. Older students may do this themselves.

Directions:

After students decide on the kind of store they want to depict, they draw and color the merchandise on paper, cut it out, put on price tags, and arrange everything in an appealing manner on the bulletin board.

When the store window is completed, young consumers may window shop for two or three items. They might write the names and prices of the items on slips of paper before adding to find out how much money is needed to buy them.

Older students may research merchandise items to gain detailed information that explains how, when, where, and why they are manufactured.

Variations:

1. For more career-related projects, see Chapter eight.
2. Store windows might display the following:

bakery goods	hardware	groceries
clothing	toys	furniture
hats	hobbies	jewelry
shoes	gifts	wallpaper
sports items	cars	photography supplies

3. Older students can become more aware of a state's tax structure by computing the amount of tax they pay for each item.

Chapter 13

Pot Pourri

BIRTHDAY CELEBRATIONS

Everyone loves birthday parties, so why not capitalize on the learning opportunities they offer while having a good time?

Materials Needed: construction paper; glitter; materials to decorate birthday cards, paper napkins, and place mats (may be paper towels): yarn, felt, foam, crayons, paint, chalk, etc.; felt to make a cake; flannel board and refreshments, if desired

Directions:

At the beginning of each month, whoever celebrates a birthday during the month places a name card (or other reminders) on a calendar around the special day.

As each date arrives, the ''birthday student'' may decorate a card holder which can easily be made from two large sheets of construction paper stapled or glued on three of the four edges. Other students make cards for the birthday student. A glittering paper crown may also be made to wear on that day. The birthday child and a friend may decorate a large felt cake (placed on the flannel board) by using yarn, interfacing, felt, and/or foam. The birthday student may also choose a game to play, and a poem or story for the teacher to read to the class.

Group birthday celebrations work well for older students. All those celebrating birthdays during a particular month are guests for part of a specified day. Parties may be set either for the fifteenth of each month or for once a semester, with a third celebration for summer birthdays just before school is out.

The following committees may be formed:

- Decorating Committee—responsible for decorating place mats, napkins, favors, and room ornaments.
- Entertainment Committee—organize and present some entertainment such as a skit, songs, a play, or a pantomine.
- Refreshment Committee—make and serve simple refreshments.
- Card Committee—design a card and write an original poem on it.

GIFT CARDS

Gift cards encourage language development and creativity, and provide an excellent opportunity for sharing inexpensive, meaningful gifts.

Materials Needed: construction paper; crayons, paints, or colored chalk

Directions:

Each child folds a piece of paper in half and decorates the outside to look like a wrapped gift. Inside, he draws a picture, or writes a story, poem, or riddle. Participants may wish to keep their gifts a secret as classmates guess what they are by asking questions that can be answered by either "yes" or "no" (e.g. Is your gift a toy? Does your gift have wheels?).

Variations.

1. The children may wish to have a gift exchange by making their gifts for specific friends. In this case, everyone who makes a gift card should receive one.
2. Placing completed gift cards in a box enables each participant to draw one at random.

3. These gifts are fun to give to a person who is leaving the school such as a student, teacher, aid, or student teacher.

MOTIVATE WITH STICKERS

Young children can often be motivated to do constructive work when their accomplishments are rewarded with stickers. Baseball cards make good incentives for older students to complete tasks.

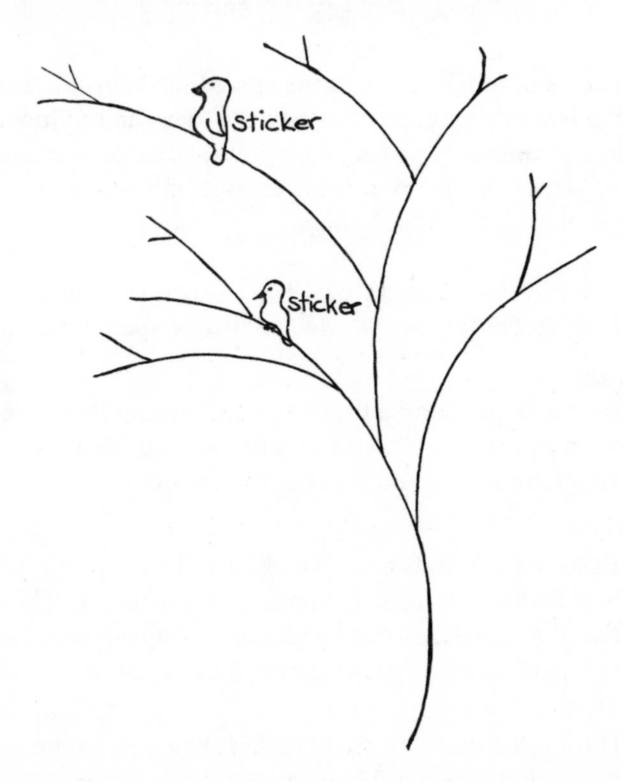

Materials Needed: stickers (such as seals or stickers made from Contact paper), paper for art projects (optional)

Preparation:

Use commercial seals or make stickers from Contact paper (some children may prefer to make them).

Directions:

Children may earn stickers after they complete a specified number of activities, such as those listed in "Spare Time Activities" in this chapter.

Children may be given seasonal stickers to use in art projects of their choice (see illustration).

Variation:

Use stickers occasionally for behavior modification rewards.

SPARE TIME ACTIVITIES

Suggestions of things to do during spare time help children stay busy with valuable learning projects. As they see ideas and follow directions, many children can think of project variations and original ideas. Teachers keep track of achievements by reading the accomplishments that students list weekly in their individual folders.

Materials Needed: a sheet of 12 x 18 inch construction paper for each student, crayons, stapler, list of spare time suggestions

Preparation:

Before duplicating a list of spare time activities, a teacher may wish to ask the class to contribute their ideas. A copy of all suggestions is then prepared for each child.

Directions:

Each student folds a sheet of 12 x 18 inch construction paper in half and decorates it for an individual folder. The duplicated list of suggestions can be placed or stapled inside it. Children may add to their list whenever they invent and exchange new ideas.

During the week students record their spare time accomplishments and give the folder to the teacher either at a conference, when projects are discussed, or on a specified day.

Weekly information can be stored in children's individual files for future evaluations and parent conferences.

The following list of spare time suggestions can be modified and expanded to meet the needs of the children:

Art:

1. Invent something from materials in the recycling box. What did you make?
2. Use a paper punch to punch small circles from paper or styrofoam cups. Use these in a creative picture or design.
3. Make picture of a person with a balloon shape above his head. Write his thoughts inside this balloon.
4. Make something from clay and describe it on paper. Place the description in your folder.
5. Design stationery and a postage stamp and then write a letter.
6. Embroider, crochet, or knit a creative design.
7. Paint a seasonal picture by the easel.
8. With your eyes closed, make a simple design on paper with a black crayon. Open your eyes and use other crayons to add to that design or make another of your choice.

Language Arts:

1. Read a story in a magazine. What story did you read? ______________________.
2. Ask someone to read a book in the hall with you.
3. Write a puppet play. Make puppet characters and have a friend help you present a puppet show.
4. Make a picture dictionary.
5. Invent a word game and teach it to your friends.
6. Dramatize seasonal poetry with a play or pantomine.
7. Make a poetry book or file by copying favorite poems and writing some of your own.
8. Practice a poem or story and record it on tape.
9. Cut out single words and pictures from magazines and newspapers. Arrange these in sentences. Glue them to a sheet of paper.
10. During activity time, act out words that begin with a certain phonetic sound (p, dr). Ask others to guess the words you are dramatizing. What are some of the words that you dramatized? ______________________

Math:

1. Measure six or more items in the room and record their size on paper. Place this record of measurement in your folder.
2. Write some mathematical stories for classmates to solve.
3. Make a calendar for either this month or next month.
4. Invent a math game and teach a friend to play it. Who played the game with you? ______________.
5. Use flash cards to practice math facts on the blackboard. How many minutes did you practice?______
6. Weigh six or more items on the scale and record their weights.
7. Write the numerals as far as you know them.
8. Make some toy money for everyone to use. Place it in your folder in a small plastic bag.
9. Cut circles, squares, and triangles from scraps of paper. Glue them on a large sheet of paper to make a design.

Science:

1. Find a science experiment on a file card or in a book and try it. Which experiment did you try?______ What did the experiment show that you didn't already know? ______________________________
2. Experiment to see what magnets attract. Make a list of these items. Make a list of things that magnets do *not* attract.
3. Use several different materials to make many boats that float. Put on a boat show in a child's wading pool, a dish pan, or in the sink.
4. Invent an ecology game. Play it with a friend. What is the name of the game? ____________________
5. Make an ecology poster, put masking tape on the back, and press it on the *east* wall.
6. Keep a list of the types of birds you see for a week.
7. Keep a record of the weather for a week. List the temperature and tell if there is any rain or snow.

Social Studies:

1. Prepare a chalk talk about a special historical event to

present to the class (this may be done for any subject).

2. Make up a play about volunteers who work in the community.
3. Interview a member of your family and a neighbor to find out about their work. Place your report or a cassette tape of the interview in the folder.
4. Write some safety slogans and practice reading them. Tape them for others to hear.
5. Research a favorite state. Write your report on an outline map of the state.
6. Make a scrapbook about one of your hobbies. The scrapbook will be laminated and placed in the library.
7. (Economics) Go on an imaginary shopping trip. Take several price tags from our tag box and find an item in the catalog whose price matches or nearly matches each tag. List on a sheet of paper the names and prices of the items you wish to buy. Add all the prices to see how much money you would spend today.

Writing:

1. Write a menu for a restaurant. Place it in your folder.
2. Write a description of something in the room. Other students can try to guess the object.
3. Write about something that happened in your neighborhood.
4. Keep a diary for a week or more.
5. Cut a picture from a magazine, glue it to a piece of paper, and write a story about it.
6. Write some riddles. Illustrate the answers.
7. Write some tongue twisters.
8. Write a shopping list of groceries (or other things) that you would like to buy at the store.
9. Write and illustrate a cartoon strip for an imaginary newspaper.
10. Make a greeting card. Draw a picture and write a verse.

Variations:

1. These activities may be used as a "choice of activities" contract or assignment. For example, the students might

be assigned to choose and complete at least two activities in each subject area within a designated length of time.

2. These activities can be used anytime to correlate with appropriate subjects.
3. See other chapters for more spare time activity ideas.

WISHING WELL

Teachers can become aware of children's individual wishes through a wishing well whose suggestions can aid in the planning of learning experiences.

Materials Needed: large ice cream containers or similar containers, laths or narrow boards, wooden dowel, nails, cord, small plastic pail or cup for bucket, paper, decorating material such as: Contact paper, wallpaper, or construction paper

Preparation:

1. Follow the illustrated directions for making a wishing well.
2. Decorate it attractively.
3. Make paper pebbles on which children can write theii wishes.

Directions:

The children write (or dictate them to an adult who will write) their wishes on the paper pebbles, sign their names, and put the pebbles in a wishing well. Wishes might include: what a child would like to do outdoors; the name of a friend with whom he would like to work; an idea for a creative project; a

Step 1- Cover the bucket with contact paper and attach lathes with nails or staples.

favorite story, song, or poem he has to share; a certain art piece he wants to display, or a particular character in a play he wishes to portray. When the teacher is prepared to make a child's wish come true, the correct paper pebble is placed in the pail, the child pulls up his note, and the wish is granted.

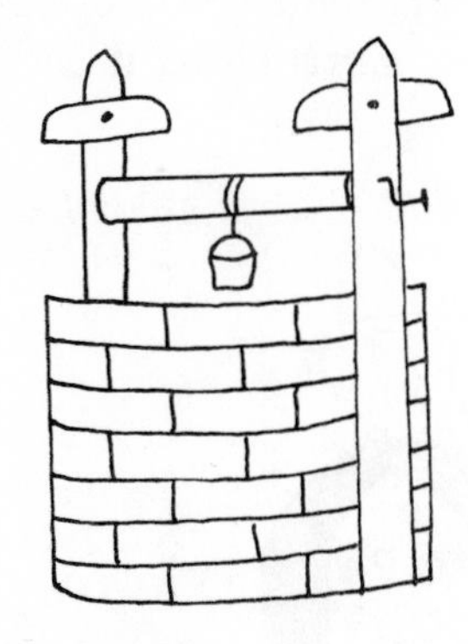

Step 2- Nail a dowel to the lathes, leaving it loose enough to turn. Bend the nail for a handle. Connect the dowel to the cup's pipe cleaner handle with yarn.

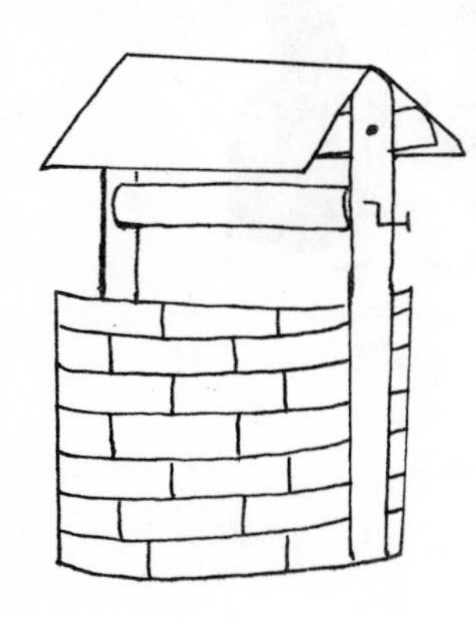

Step 3- Bend a piece of cardboard to form a roof, decorate it as desired and attach it to the lathes.

WORLDLY VOLUNTEERS (IMAGINARY)

These paper plate people from other lands volunteer to tell students about their countries via the tape recorder.

Materials Needed: tape and tape recorder or cassette and cassette recorder, paper plates, cardboard tubes from the inside of wrapping or waxed paper, books about people from other countries, scraps of paper, old clothing or fabric to make clothing (interfacing), a puppet holder (made from a dowel glued on a wooden base)—optional

Preparation:

1. Cut a slot in the back of one tube so that the tubes can be interlocked and glued as shown in the illustrations.
2. Design and dress the puppet to resemble a native of the country he represents.
3. The teacher or an older student gathers and tapes information about people from other lands, narrating as if each puppet is telling the story.

Older students can do the preparation with teacher guidance.

Directions:

Paper plate volunteers take turns sitting beside the tape recorder to tell about their countries. Children may listen alone or in groups. Students who wish to participate in this activity can do the necessary research and make their own puppets and tapes either individually or with friends.

Variations:

1. Make holiday puppets, such as a witch to tell a Halloween story.
2. Make story characters to go with classics or with the children's creative writing.
3. Use these paper plate characters in creative puppet shows

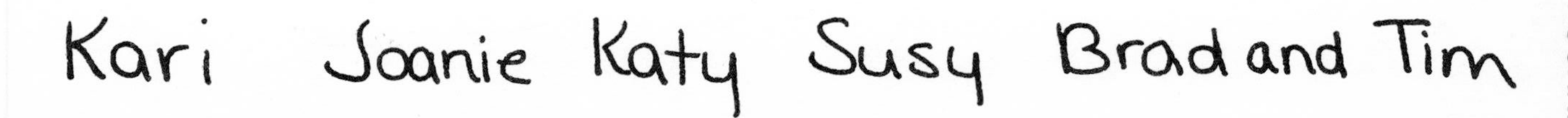
Kari Joanie Katy Susy Brad and Tim

Index

F

G

H

I

J

K

L

T

V

W

Y